TRADITION AND CHANGE
IN ENGLISH LIBERAL EDUCATION

Tradition and Change in English Liberal Education

An Essay in History and Culture

SHELDON ROTHBLATT

FABER AND FABER
3 Queen Square, London WC1

First published in 1976
by Faber and Faber Limited
3 Queen Square London WC1
Printed in Great Britain by
Latimer Trend & Company Ltd Plymouth

ISBN 0 571 10574 2

Contents

Preface

———

THE ESSAY that follows is different in procedure and emphasis but not in purpose from the work of the late Professor Joseph Levenson, who wrote on the meaning of Confucian ideals for modern China. I, too, am interested in the nature of the transmission of cultural values over long periods of time and in whether historical continuity can be expected of the collections of beliefs we sometimes call 'tradition'. One often hears of the influence or tyranny of the past over the present or complaints of how difficult it is to change ideas and institutions once they are established. Certainly received values often appear to be in conflict with desires for change, but I would still maintain that there is a tendency to over-simplify the meaning of a tradition and to misconstrue its influence. In order to elaborate this conclusion and to point out its consequences, I have examined the history of English liberal education as one example of a tradition that is well known and referred to continually. I find that liberal education has been so closely associated with particular historical contexts that it has not really survived them, except as an idea and perhaps as an ideology.

Liberal education is of particular concern to technological societies because as specialism proceeds, liberal education seems to dispute the advance and even to fall victim to it. I have inquired into the ways this may or may not be true. I have also tried to understand why it is that liberal education has always been so difficult to define and why its declared or presumed ends have been virtually unattainable. The answer lies in the uses of education. Throughout much of its modern history liberal education has been utilitarian, although concerned less with the direct preparation for occupations than for the active life. The

9

antithesis is not as great as it appears, however. Conduct and career have not always been easy to separate. Often the two have been entangled, giving rise, as I hope to illustrate, to moral ambiguity or contradiction. For all ideas, whether educational or not, are caught in distinct value structures created by historical circumstances, and it is difficult to see how, in view of the changing complexity of society over time, moral ambiguity or contradictions in conduct can be avoided. It is also worth remembering that each society or age creates new expressions of ambiguity and unique forms of tension, especially as idea is fitted to circumstance and theory to practice. How tensions are contained or released in different historical periods is also discussed in this essay.

The word 'culture' as used in the subtitle and throughout the essay is meant to underlie and reinforce the use of the word 'history'. Liberal education frequently has been explicitly moral or socio-moral. It has made living in the world an end. 'Culture' —values implied or expressed in behaviour—is therefore the appropriate word to describe the many and subtle interpenetrations of history, society, and education.

The materials for a study of liberal education are staggering, and the concepts and ideas available for organizing the materials rich and various. It would certainly be difficult to cover every aspect of the history of liberal education in England, and so I have selected those sources and examples central to my theme and presentation. The essay may be said to have two interlocking sections. The first is a detailed inquiry into the leading characteristics of liberal education as it developed in Georgian England. The second pursues the history (or fate) of eighteenth-century values as expressed in education through new historical and institutional situations in the centuries following. My interest throughout is in establishing a correspondence between culture and education and in explaining their mutual interaction.

While my thoughts took form, colleagues and friends contributed to them by raising qualifications and by adding their perspective. Berkeley historians and friends—Wolfgang Sauer, Roger Hahn, Irwin Scheiner, and Robert Middlekauff—have each of them given me time, thought, and the benefit of their learning. Murray Cohen has shared with me on numerous occasions his understanding of eighteenth-century literature,

Preface

and Robert Brown, a physicist who can remember what a liberal education should be, has been a steady influence during the writing of this book. Conversations with my colleague William Bouwsma were invaluable. His reflections on education and culture in western civilization have greatly improved my comprehension of certain basic lines of development. To my friend A. H. Halsey, Professorial Fellow of Nuffield College, Oxford, and Head of the Department of Social and Administrative Studies, I owe many debts, among them the support he gave me when my work was in its initial stage. Without his encouragement, the writing would not have proceeded so rapidly. I owe special thanks to J. M. Newton of Clare College, Cambridge, for lending me his doctoral dissertation on the development of English studies in British universities. It arrived at just the right moment to aid my thinking, and I am grateful to Lord Ashby, Master of Clare College, for suggesting it and for his kindnesses in the past. Professor David Spring of Johns Hopkins has sent me several suggestions, and I would like to thank him for having read an earlier version of this essay. Dame Lucy Sutherland, Principal of Lady Margaret Hall, Oxford, who has not yet seen this book, was helpful to me in ways she may not remember. I would like to thank her for the pleasure of a summer's talk. Brian Harrison of Corpus Christi College, Oxford, arranged for my stay in Corpus when the idea for the essay grew, and I would like to record my gratitude for his thoughtfulness. Susan Kennedy and Matthew Evans of Faber and Faber have been very kind in many ways, and they, too, deserve my thanks.

The financial support I received while writing was instrumental in seeing that my work came to fruition. Without the assistance of the John Simon Guggenheim Memorial Foundation in New York, the Institute of International Studies, the Humanities Faculty Fellowship Program, and the Department of History of the University of California, Berkeley, I would not have been able to complete the project. For source material I am grateful to the Master and Fellows of Balliol College, Oxford, for use of the Jenkyns Papers, to the kindness of Dr. J. F. A. Mason, Librarian of Christ Church, Oxford, for making the Chinnery Papers accessible, and the Governing Body of Christ Church for permission to use them.

Finally, I would like to record my three greatest obligations.

11

Preface

The first is to my wife Barbara for hours of critical assistance. The second is to my old friend George Stocking of the University of Chicago. He subjected my drafts to an uncompromising scrutiny and brought his stunning logical ability to bear on the discussion. He entered completely into the spirit of the argument itself and made numerous suggestions for changes in structure and thought. He also—will he be surprised to read it?—brought civility into my life.

The third obligation is inspirational. It is to my first and greatest teacher, my brother Ben, to whom these pages are dedicated. 'To me'—I use the words of the novelist I. B. Singer about his brother I. J. Singer—'he was not only the older brother, but a spiritual father and master as well. I looked up to him always as to a model of high morality and literary honesty. Although a modern man, he had all the great qualities of our pious ancestors.'

Berkeley, California, 1974.

I

Introduction

WE MUST write on problems not periods, said Lord Acton; but in fact we do both, hoping to find that problems fill up and define an age. Only in this way do we have markers along the historical road to the present. England in the eighteenth century is set off from an earlier age in many ways: in politics, in economic life and development, in the character of life lived in cities, in music and in the changing English language, spoken or written. So, too, is it set off from an earlier age in the structure, meaning, definition and implications of what was called then, was called before it, and is still called 'a liberal education'.

The phrase 'a liberal education' is of ancient origin, whether we mean liberal arts or liberal sciences. In the seventeenth century there was still a distinction between the two forms of liberal education, although they were complementary. Arts were more instrumental, having to do with the preparation and training of the intellect. Sciences were subjects studied for the knowledge they provided. Logic and rhetoric—the latter very broadly conceived to include all possible ideas and sources of communication—were arts subjects, while theology, jurisprudence, medicine, and philosophy were liberal sciences.[1] These were the meanings of the words arts and sciences as used in the scholastic or Aristotelian vocabulary; but by 1750 they were being used differently, and in one respect at least, interchangeably. As the author of *Observations upon Liberal Education, in All Its Branches* remarks: 'Instruction in the science or art of right living, is the chief lesson in education, to which all others ought to be rendered subservient; and what this science is, and

[1] William T. Costello, *The Scholastic Curriculum at Early Seventeenth-Century Cambridge* (Cambridge, Mass., 1958), Chapters II and III.

13

what may justly be called false learning.'[1] Whether art or science, the emphasis must be on living rather than on knowing.

Ideas and ideals of a liberal education descended into modern times from the days of the university *quadrivium* and *trivium*, from the *studium generale*, but only in part. For essentially they entered England as they did Northern Europe from the humanists of Renaissance Italy, taking hold here and there in the kingdom during the sixteenth and seventeenth centuries but not bursting forth until the eighteenth century. They then became a wonderful reinforcement, indeed a carrier, of changes in social and cultural values.

I lay some weight on the delayed impact of the Renaissance. Superficially, at least, the full force of Continental influence does not seem apparent in England until long after the principles of a liberal education appeared abroad. This is by no means the place to reopen a perhaps fruitless controversy over whether England experienced an Italian Renaissance in the Age of Henry and Elizabeth; but no student of the later history can fail to notice the deep influence of cinquecento models and forms in the social and cultural history of Georgian England. Huge pedimental façades; octagonal shapes employed at Chiswick by Lord Burlington and repeated in the design of George I coffee-pots; the Italian masters of all periods, and Flemings as well; discourses on political science modelled on the writings of great Florentines; the appearance of a secular, individualist auto-biographical genre in the middle of the eighteenth century—the list of influences can be extended and should be. For England in the late seventeenth century and throughout the eighteenth century was a great borrower and unashamedly so. The brilliant culture of Renaissance and Baroque Europe lay before it, to be combined with its own brilliant contributions to scientific thought and constitutionalism. Charles Wilson has recorded other obligations the English owed the Continent. England in the seventeenth and eighteenth centuries was greatly indebted to the Low Countries for major economic assistance, for inno-vations in the carrying out of commerce and mercantile business, and in the establishment of instruments for promoting private and public finance. The Dutch pioneered the fisheries industry,

[1] George Turnbull, *Observations upon Liberal Education, In All Its Branches* (London, 1742), xi.

invented 'flyboats' for cheap freightage in North Sea waters, and pointed the way towards agricultural change. There were debts to Holland of another kind. When Hogarth paints himself, for example, an amused Rembrandt peers back.

The contributions of seventeenth-century France must be acknowledged, for these were known and appreciated in England despite the Francophobia that closed one century and opened another. Not only were French literary and artistic achievements admired, but London Englishmen, coming to terms with the 'wen' for virtually the first time, were uncomfortably aware of their cultural inferiority compared to the French. They believed themselves less adept at the arts and pleasures of social life; and although it diminished, the belief did not vanish until the French Revolution. The reign of Louis XIV produced an elaborate code of conduct that radiated outwards from Versailles, comprehending those niceties of behaviour or those gestures of face and body that were once called etiquette and that some now call kinesic.[1] The English court in the reigns of Charles II and James II lacked the high formality, regulation, and carefully prescribed ceremonies of the French one. It consisted of a jumble of competing, noisy interests, with no single channel of communication to the crown.[2] Once again, Continental models of conduct, rules, or codes of behaviour arrived in England belatedly, long after they had been formulated abroad, to be absorbed into a social structure and political constitution that did not resemble any across the Channel. In the middle of the eighteenth century, while new conquests were being made in the fairest corners of the earth, and the Jacobitism finally disappeared which had nagged away at the United Kingdom of England, Scotland, and Ireland for nearly half a century, Englishmen, taking pride in a settled constitution and a happy realm, could also point to improvements in interpersonal behaviour and in the relationships of men to women. For many of them, at least, these ranked nearly as high as the political and economic achievements. In retrospect we can see that all the changes, whether cultural, political, or economic, were interrelated, each supposing or in some way promoting the other.

All the historical changes occurring in the course of the

[1] Erving Goffman.
[2] J. R. Jones, *The Revolution of 1688 in England* (London, 1972), 18–28.

eighteenth century bore significantly upon the meaning of a liberal education. Ends, means, social and moral uses, values arising in different sources for different purposes—all became confused or, perhaps more accurately, assumed new meaning from unfamiliar juxtaposition, like the adjacent colours of the contemporary painter, Josef Albers. The enculturating aspects of education were never more in evidence than in the later eighteenth century. And crucial to the entire process of preparing young persons for the parts they were to take on in the world at large were the moral presuppositions underlying changing standards of personal and interpersonal behaviour. There is no greater cultural contrast between the eighteenth century and later periods than in the degree to which the ideals of a liberal education were central to standards of correct or proper social conduct and notions of ethical self-improvement. The history of a liberal education in Georgian England is truly a history of 'the science or art of right living'. It is the history of socio-moral conduct. It goes without saying that in the eighteenth century, as in any century, such conduct was historically conditioned. We need to inquire, therefore, into the historical reasons for the forms of moral behaviour emerging in Georgian society. To do so we must discuss at the outset a number of key words, phrases, or concepts, all of them in active use in the period itself.

2

Civilization

THE FIRST word is 'civilization'. In the eighteenth century the word did not mean what it means to Lord Clark—specifically, the artistic achievements of mankind, especially architecture. This view of the importance of art, which also presupposes the autonomy of art and its independence from morality, was emerging at the very end of the eighteenth century; but its proper history is much later in the next century. 'Civilization' was a more comprehensive and even ethical term, designating all those material or institutional, but particularly those religious, moral, or intellectual, changes that separated the tame European from the wild barbarian. Civilization was the release from involuntary responses such as instinct or unconscious controls such as custom[1] to conscious obligations and specified freedoms. However, the release from inhibitions outside one's control implied an even greater responsibility to impose new ones from within, and ultimately civilization meant control over oneself through the use of reason, judgement, and understanding. It meant self-restraint for a twofold purpose: defensively against provocation, and in deference to the wishes of others. Civilization was indeed, as Freud said it was, self-repression, and its object he also approved of: the reduction of violence and cruelty, whether to animals or to people. If the Georgians were interested in hunting, at least they understood that badger-baiting was uncivilized and goose-riding barbarous. And if they were snobbish and self-indulgent, at least they knew that the highest forms of rational behaviour were courtesy and concern for

[1] George W. Stocking, Jr., *Race, Culture and Evolution* (New York, 1968), 318.

17

others. Even a peer had an obligation to be respectful or con-
descending to those below him. A democratic age such as ours
is easily offended by condescension; but we must not at least let
one historical nuance escape us. Condescension—'voluntary
humiliation' and the 'descent from superiority', as Dr. Johnson
defined the word—acquires a much different meaning, a more
active one, in a society with hierarchical groupings. The ethical
obligation is greater.

'Civilization' was a higher state of response, not merely
material—international trade, cities, elegant houses, parks,
theatres, comfort—but profoundly moral, having to do with the
way in which men and women treated themselves, treated one
another, and even treated animals. That 'civilization' could
receive this special kind of emphasis will be clearer if we realize
that it was not the only word the eighteenth century possessed
to describe an improved, a better, and a higher state of human
conduct. Its special meaning was in fact forced on it etymo-
logically and culturally.

'Civilization' was late on the historical scene, a neologism of
the sixth and seventh decades of eighteenth-century Europe.
It was the substantive form of 'to civilize', which had been
available all along and continued in use. 'Some Nations are
fiery and hasty, others slow and phlegmatick; some are of a
sweet nature and civiliz'd, when others are wild and not
sociable.'[1] Thus Jean Gailhard in 1678. 'Civilization' emerged
only after a long search to express a particular stage of European
history, sometimes the final or ultimate stage. The word appeared
first in France, according to the conclusions of a delightful
symposium conducted in France in 1930.[2] It came into English
from Scotland, where a group of intellectuals, anxious to bring
their country into the mainstream of European intellectual
progress, launched a series of brilliant inquiries into the whole
meaning of civilized behaviour. An older use of civilization,
vaguely related to the newer meaning, had been known on
both sides of the Channel but was rapidly disappearing. 'Civilization' had been a legal term derived from 'civil'. Johnson defined

[1] Jean Gailhard, *The Compleat Gentleman: or Directions for the Education of Youth as to their Breeding at Home and Travelling Abroad* (London,
1678), 72.
[2] George Lefebvre, ed., *Civilisation—le mot et l'idée* (Paris, 1930).

it in 1755 in the first edition of his Dictionary as 'a law, act of justice, or judgment which renders a criminal process civil'. But it was eliminated by the time the ninth edition appeared some thirty-five years later. Before there was 'civilization', there were *'policer'* and *'politesse'* in France, 'refinement', 'politeness', and 'civility' (from *civilité*) in England, but all with narrower or ambiguous meanings, at least no meaning that provided an unmistakable reference to the benefits of reason. In the second half of the seventeenth century the great statesman and historian, Edward Hyde, Earl of Clarendon, related the word 'Civility' to 'good Manners', as in the passage, 'whatsoever is of Civility and good Manners, all that is of Art and Beauty, or of real and solid Wealth in the World, is the . . . child of beloved Propriety [meaning property]',[1] and from this apposition the eighteenth century could not escape, although the urge to do so was always present. A pamphlet of 1728 speaks of the 'Politeness and Civility of Europe' in the twofold but here connected sense of manners and improvement, of 'refining the *Modern* Taste'.[2] In a famous conversation of 1772 Johnson refused to admit the neologistic meaning of civilization into his Dictionary. He preferred 'civility' and used it, in fact, in describing the moral changes in Scotland he noticed when visiting the Hebrides. 'With great deference to him,' wrote Boswell, 'I thought *civilization*, from to *civilize* better in the sense opposed to *barbarity*, than *civility*; as it is better to have a distinct word for each sense, than one word with two senses, which *civility* is, in his way of using it.'[3]

But not only in his way. 'Civility' was a fully nuanced word in the eighteenth century. It could be used very narrowly in the plural to refer to the various forms of social entertainment and entertaining—'Civilities of this sort', as in an essay first published in 1727.[4] Or with a touch less of pure pleasure and a shade more courtesy and thoughtfulness, in which sense we find it in 1789

[1] Quoted in Christopher Hill, *Puritanism and Revolution* (New York, 1970), 211.
[2] William Hirst, *The Necessity and Advantages of Education* (London, 1728), 16–17.
[3] James Boswell, *Life of Samuel Johnson* (London, 1966), 466.
[4] *The Expence of University Education Reduced*, 2nd ed. (London, 1733), 13. British Museum 731.h.4(4).

as in the phrase: 'that stern independence . . . which recoils
against the blandishments of praise, and shrinks at the soothings
of condolence; annihilates the elegances, the civilities, the
diversions of life, and . . . renders our manners rough and perhaps our hearts unfeeling.'[1] In the singular, the word was used
to indicate decency and the effort made to avoid being rude, but
directed towards a specific personal advantage, as in this senten-
tious line from 1730: 'Depend upon it, Good-nature and
Civility will by degrees gain the Love of all, and will make you
very easy amongst your Companions.'[2] The same self-regarding
objective but in the negative form of the word is mentioned in
this early nineteenth-century advice from a mother to her son
at Oxford: 'You might occasionally, when ever you think it
worth while, steal a quarter of an hour from the wine of your
own set, in order to accept another invitation, expressing always
"much regret at leaving them for a few minutes in order to
escape the charge of incivility." '[3] Yet another example, this
time from 1773, with still another edge to the meaning: civility
as the respect exchanged between social equals, implying an
even stronger obligation than if the relationship were between
persons of unequal standing. In speaking of his Oxford fellowship, Richard Radcliffe wrote to a friend that 'It enabled me to
go into the company of my superiors with the greater pleasure,
because I was not dependent upon them, and made me be
received with the greater civility by them, because they knew I
wanted nothing from them.'[4]

Both specific and general forms—the civility due to a particular
person or civility as a general standard of correct social behaviour—in both singular and plural occur frequently in the
writings of Jane Austen; but let this example from *Mansfield
Park*, which appeared in print in 1814, suffice to catch the sense
of painful personal duty inching toward a higher obligation: 'I

[1] *The Loiterer*, 12 September 1789 (Oxford, 1790), 4.

[2] Daniel Waterland, *Advice to a Young Student, with a Method of
Study for the Four First Years* (London, 1730), 6.

[3] George Robert Chinnery Papers, Christ Church Library, Oxford,
19 October 1808.

[4] Margaret Evans, ed., *Letters of Richard Radcliffe and John James of
Queen's College, Oxford, 1755–1783* (Oxford, 1888), 31.

am worn out with civility, said he. I have been talking incessantly all night, and with nothing to say.'[1]

It is easy to see why Boswell wanted civilization to replace civility. An important word was desperately needed to break the hold that manners held on poor burdened civility. A neologism sharp and fresh was required to describe the long climb out of a state of brutal nature into the spacious eighteenth century, to designate a cultural goal and at the same time celebrate the attainment of it. Even Thomas Paine, whose *Rights of Man* treats of the most important political questions of the day, could find no other word to summarize Edmund Burke's attack on the Jacobin revolution in France than civility, straining its use even more. 'Among the incivilities by which nations or individuals provoke and irritate each other,' begins the famous treatise, 'Mr. Burke's pamphlet on the French Revolution is an extraordinary instance.'[2] Here ideological conflict and high international politics are reduced to a breach of manners, as if states were persons engaged in tasteless insult. Indeed, the parallel between nations and individuals is explicit.

The persistent strain of primitivism that we find in eighteenth-century thought, implying the return to a simpler and happier state, and the increasing influence of Greek theories of degeneration and decline do not invalidate the Georgian belief that reason would lift mankind out of barbarism. Optimism and hope are never far from despair. The more a particular cultural goal becomes urgent, the more likely is the mind to dwell on the possibilities of relapse and the greater becomes the desire to break the fall. Sensitive minds of the eighteenth century were very much aware how dark were the sources of human conduct, how easy it was for man to lapse, and how great and frequent were the temptations to do so.

'Civilization' did not immediately replace 'civility'. And this is of the greatest importance in our attempt to recover the meaning of a liberal education in the later eighteenth century. For it means that the end of a liberal education was something less than civilization and something more than civility. It is impor-

---

[1] Jane Austen, *Mansfield Park* (Harmondsworth, 1972), 283, also 231, 235.

[2] Thomas Paine, *The Rights of Man* (Garden City, New York, 1961), 275. Professor George Stocking called my attention to this reference.

tant to bear in mind that civility is a word that reaches towards civilization. It is an open-ended word continually pointing beyond itself, like the baroque ellipse of Nikolaus Pevsner's description. The conduct it describes is always more important than the examples to which it refers. What to us may be no more than fashionable trivialities or social conventions and mere surface behaviour are certainly that. But at the same time they are also something else, something greater, echoes and reminders that higher ideals are always present in what Johnson called the 'minuter decencies and inferior duties' necessary 'to regulate the practice of daily conversation, to correct those depravities which are rather ridiculous than criminal, and remove those grievances which, if they produce no lasting calamities, impress hourly vexation.'[1] The aim of civilization and civilized behaviour was neither superficial nor superficially sought. It was not, as we are tempted to accuse, complacent. Even the smallest improvement in daily relations, for example, the decline in raillery, crudeness, and cavil, all symptoms of violence, could be legitimately considered a major accomplishment.

A postscript for the historical record: civility reached towards civilization but did not realize its ultimate aspiration. In the nineteenth century civility fell back to its original lesser meanings after what has to be called a memorable, brave try.

---

[1] Samuel Johnson, *Lives of the Poets*, I (London, 1964), 407.

3
Liberal

═══════

How to be civilized was the central preoccupation of eighteenth-century thinkers, whether French, Scottish, or English. The conscious improvement of morals and manners was never far from the daily thoughts of divines, novelists, philosophers, political economists, poets, or painters. And because they believed that they and their countries were involved in an historic effort to push upward out of barbarism, they were inclined to look upon their times as an 'age' with distinct characteristics. In England from the later days of the Restoration right through the eighteenth century and even beyond, writers and thinkers tended to give labels to their periods, to call them an Augustan Age, or an age of progress, enlightenment, or betterment. Some standard of achievement was assumed or advocated, even though in counterpoint pessimists played another theme: the only measurable progress, they chided, was in the refinement of cruelty. Others complained that enlightenment was nothing more than an excuse for luxury and indulgence. As it is by no means the rule in history that the majority of an educated part of society believes in an historic role, the concern for linear periodization deserves our attention. It does so especially because the belief became commonplace that 'civilized' behaviour could be learned if it were taught, that the rational mind, once awakened to the meaning of civilization, would readily grasp its benefits. Thus arose opportunities that pedagogues did not let slip. Writings on the purpose and forms of liberal education proliferated in the eighteenth century, for above all a liberal education was the pathway to civilization.

In eighteenth-century England the word 'liberal' meant free—that is, it still carried with it one of the connotations of ancient Greek usage. Liberal was related to liberate and freedom. A liberal education was the education suited to a freeman. But in Greek times there were also slaves, and so the opposite of liberal was servile. The fundamental division between freeman and slave within the Hellenic polis underlay every other consideration of privilege or responsibility, social or civic. A liberal education automatically presupposed a particular social condition, one that was largely accidental.

To the enlightened mind of Europe, slavery was a barbarous practice, repugnant to every civilized man or woman. Educated Englishmen wrote against it, as did Scots. Johnson toasted 'the next rebellion of the Negroes in the West Indies'.[1] John Millar closed his classic account of the origins of social distinctions with the lofty statement that the condemnation of slavery by the chief court in Scotland in 1778 'may be accounted an authentic testimony of the liberal sentiments entertained in the latter part of the eighteenth century'.[2] No distinction between slave and freeman, therefore, can indicate the underlying social condition presupposed in the idea of a liberal education in the eighteenth century. Yet there remained a carry-over from ancient Greek usage in the word liberal as encountered in the eighteenth century, although a highly ambiguous one. The notion of some sort of social superiority inherent in the recipient of a liberal education was never wholly absent in common thought. Accident continued to play a part in deciding who should receive a liberal education and who a servile or, as it was called, 'mechanical' one. Birth and privilege undoubtedly imparted an advantage; but luck, circumstances, and determination were by no means to be ruled out.

There was a hard reality to be faced by the person desiring a liberal education. A liberal education was far too expensive for most people. Not only were expenses—to include all kinds of miscellaneous fees and boarding if required—too high; there was the additional problem of the costs of deferred employment in an age when early entry into the job market was the rule. It was easily concluded that those unable to expend a certain amount of money on a liberal education were of low origin. It was expected and widely accepted as an irreversible fact of social

[1] Quoted in 'Augustinianism, Authoritarianism, Anthropolatry', *Eighteenth-Century Studies*, V (Spring, 1972), 458.

[2] John Millar, *The Origin of the Distinction of Ranks* (Basel, 1793), 284.

life that the greater majority of those born to families of low status in society would never be able to rise very high.

The interesting question of the social basis of Georgian education can be examined in several contexts. If we return for a moment to the England of the Stuarts, we can see that in educational terms at least the words 'liberal' and 'servile' were not adamantly opposed. In the scholastic university curriculum of early seventeenth-century Cambridge both liberal and servile kinds of education existed, each responsible for different functions but joining to form complementary components of the arts curriculum. According to the Thomistic educational schema still actively used, servile arts (of the body) were practical—agriculture, for example, or painting; liberal arts (of the mind) were intellectual—logic and rhetoric.[1] But in the eighteenth century the arts of the body separated from the arts of the mind, and servile came to be regarded as an inferior form of education and unsuited to persons of gentlemanly status. The author of an early eighteenth-century dictionary, whose primary purpose is to show how language can be used to discern which nations are polite and civilized and which are not, draws a hard and fast line between liberal arts or sciences—'such as are fit for Gentlemen and Scholars'—and other forms of education—'Mechanick Trades and Handicrafts', suited for 'meaner People'. 'Servile' he defines as belonging to servants or to bondage: 'slavish, mean, pitiful, base'.[2] He thus makes a distinct association of liberal education with superior social standing.

Dr. Johnson, in defining the word 'liberal' in his Dictionary, is more elusive. His first definition links two, perhaps three or four, different cultural, psychological, or social traits. He says liberal is 'not mean; not low in birth; not low in mind'. This trilogy cannot be confidently read as if it forms a progression, and perhaps it does Johnson a disservice to think that the definitions are associated as closely as their appearance suggests. Yet from other eighteenth-century usage it is certain that 'not low in mind' is not completely separate from 'not low in birth' or 'not mean'. Henry Fielding, for example, wrote that he had 'scarce ever seen in men of low birth and education' that

[1] Costello, 37–8.
[2] N. Bailey, *An Universal Etymological English Dictionary*, 7th ed. (London, 1735).

'liberality of spirit' which he deemed essential to the nobility of men; but he also said that low-born persons were well-bred if they were good-natured. Lord Chesterfield was, as might be expected, far less generous.[1]

Unquestionably, then, the costs of education and the facts of social mobility had a decisive influence on the meanings words like 'liberal' and 'liberal education' possessed in Georgian society. Liberal education was a gentleman's education, and liberal described gentlemanly qualities. But it would be a great disservice to the history of the period to allow the matter to rest so easily. For there are contradictions in Fielding's statements, and there is an ambiguity in Johnson's definition, a confusion of qualities attributable to social status, or to mind and character, or to the importance of having and using a full purse. The confusion arises directly from a particular historical situation where the highest social prestige still adhered to an hereditary aristocracy and yet no absolute distinction could be drawn between superior and inferior, between birth and obscure origin.

Georgian society, particularly London society, was dynamic, enterprising, and challenging. Wealth was widely distributed and opportunities for social advancement plentiful. Young men who were neither of good family nor of parvenu parents could still afford a liberal education. This is one level of fact. A second concerns the actual nature and purpose of liberal education. The measure of a liberal education was social. Liberal education was concerned with definable ends and with visible qualities of character. The proof of a liberal education lay in behaviour, expressed as style, taste, fashion, or manners. This means that liberal education was not exclusive, even if it was snobbish. It was possible for many persons of humble or inferior birth to acquire the exterior polish implicit in the meaning of the phrase 'liberal education', and how high the polish required depended entirely on the social circle that was sought. Polite education may well be a class doctrine, as historians and sociologists often say it is; but in the eighteenth century it was far more than that. Polite education was utilitarian. It softened class differences in such a way as to enable some degree of social mobility to take

---

[1] C. J. Rawson, *Henry Fielding and the Augustan Ideal under Stress* (London, 1972), 27, also 24.

place. If it produced social anxieties of one kind, it relieved those of another. In time behaviour, not origin, was a sign of quality. A coarse mind still implied a low person, but not necessarily one whose social origins were inferior.

In the second half of the eighteenth century there is a subtle but noticeable shift in one of the underlying connotations of the word 'liberal'. Freedom, or the attitudes demonstrated in being free, shifts to 'independence'. Of course, independence had for some time been the hallmark of certain categories of Englishmen —groups like the proud and prosperous yeomanry of Kent, members of Parliament like Namier's Shropshire country gentlemen, and naturally the gentry everywhere. Independence defined the tradition of parliamentary representation that Burke invoked when he addressed the Bristol electors in 1774. In these examples independence inhered in the political system which, if it included the deference owed superiors by inferiors, also stressed and promoted mutual respect. Independence had been defined in essentially political terms since at least the mid seventeenth century. Independence meant a place in the complicated, unreformed franchise, which itself partook of a still older legal definition of independence as a 'liberty', a territory or privilege granted by custom, charter, or law—the famous 'Liberty of Bury St. Edmund's', for example. All these older ideas and arrangements expressed in varying measure contractual freedoms, mutually benefiting political exchanges.

As an ideal and as a reality, the belief in the importance and value of independence was constantly frustrated in the eighteenth century. The yeomanry saw their independence attacked by changes in the structure of farming. The gentry saw theirs compromised in the electoral take-over by the peerage which occurred earlier. The emergence of new potential electorates in the later eighteenth century disturbed the old system of political relationships. Each time traditional relationships were upset— and they were upset often in a century of continuous social movement—an effort was made to achieve some new version of independence. As Georgian society was so interpenetrated with different authority relationships, this was difficult to arrange. A single individual might well be both dependent and independent at one and the same time. The parish priest indebted to a lay patron for his living would certainly find himself in a dependent position; but although subservient to the squire, he nevertheless enjoyed some measure of independence from his bishop.[1]

The sinecure was the favourite mode of achieving independence in the heyday of the patronage system. The Georgian practice of converting employment into sinecures transformed jailkeepers into entrepreneurs, government clerks into freeholders, and Oxford fellows into holders of fees simple. It may be a practice repugnant to all believers in merit and efficiency, but in an age of toadying and self-seeking it produced undoubted benefits. If successful, the search for place yielded economic security and therefore self-esteem—the two were inseparably connected. Place-hunting is too well known a phenomenon of Georgian social and political life to require much comment here, but we can at least allow one Georgian time to explain the importance of a sinecure to him. Richard Radcliffe, the same Fellow of Queen's College, Oxford from whom we heard earlier, wrote in 1773 that 'It is generally allowed that indigence and dependence have an unfavourable influence both on the temper and genius of mankind. . . . That a man should be less studious or serious, less able or willing to improve himself, because he is easy and happy in his circumstances, is a doctrine I cannot comprehend.' Radcliffe spoke from bitter personal experience. 'As a Foundation man, I have been remarkably unlucky: it was nineteen years compleat, before I arrived at a Fellowship: and I am now advancing in my thirtieth year, without having had the offer of any preferment from College.' Recalling that matters could have been even worse, Radcliffe paused to express gratitude for his fellowship and in so doing stated the central reason for its importance. 'It has been the grand comfort of my life—it enabled me to go into the company of my superiors with the greatest pleasure, because I was not dependent upon them.'[2]

As the traditional political independence of many members of enfranchised groups was compromised in the eighteenth century, the search for social independence accelerated. The definition of independence broadened to take in the newly-developing concept of civilized behaviour and all the attributes

[1] An example provided by G. E. Mingay, *English Landed Society in the Eighteenth Century* (London, 1963), 149.
[2] Evans, 30–1.

of a liberally-educated man. A liberal education might not be able to guarantee social independence, but at least it gave a plausible veneer of success to its recipient, allowed him to speak with some authority, and gave him a welcome push in the right direction.

Some groups found their independence compromised. But the status of others improved, especially after 1750. For them, movement upward in the social scale was not as important as horizontal mobility, which liberal education enhanced: either concealing social origins or widening status differences. New occupations arose as a consequence of industrialism but still more as the result of the commercial and mercantile expansion that preceded it. There was an improvement in status in the arts, in publishing, in certain branches of the law, in medicine, architecture, interior decoration, in theatre scenery design, to a lesser extent in acting—at least London acting, as the status of the provincial stage failed to advance to the same degree. Today these occupations are identified as professions, but in the middle of the eighteenth century they were either trades or close to being trades. Essential to their elevation in status was a certain amount of occupational differentiation. London actors had to separate themselves from actors in the provinces, physicians from surgeons, and surgeons from barbers. Painters began to separate themselves from artisans or craftsmen, claiming that theirs was a liberal and not a servile profession, thus breaking the association between painting and the servile arts developed in the scholastic curriculum. The word 'tradesman' was coined, a neologism to designate an activity distinct from that of the artisan, who was both primary producer and seller. For each of these groups manuals or guides to proper conduct were being written, as if to underscore the novelty and uncertainty of their practice. A book written for tradesmen in the 1740s discussed *inter alia* how to assist a lady in the descent from her carriage and suggested turning discreetly away if she should (inadvertently) show her ankle.[1] Sprinkled throughout the manuals and guides can be found many of the educational sentiments expressed in treatises and essays on a liberal education written by tutors and schoolmasters, who frequently offered educational advice to men in commerce and business.

[1] R. Campbell, *The London Tradesman* (London, 1747), 147.

Before concluding this section, it is necessary to mention one other associated meaning of 'liberal' that has thus far been omitted from the discussion, a meaning that had always troubled the advocates of a liberal education. We remember that a liberal education meant a liberated, free mind. It was assumed that the real threat to society lay in the unliberated, the prejudiced, twisted mind, not free from barbarism. So happy a conclusion was comforting, but it did not solve every problem. For the same minds that joined 'liberated' and 'liberty' with liberal also connected 'licence' to it. 'Luxury, licence, and misrule have been introduced in the train of liberty,' said the physician Richard Davies.[1] Blackstone, in his famous lectures on law, spoke about the 'licentiousness of politer life'.[2] It was indeed an ingenious paradox, and it troubled as well as fascinated the Georgians, whether at home or abroad on the grand tour. In Venice, as William Bouwsma has written, the Englishman could view the paradox in its most brilliant international setting. The political liberty of Venice, her political principles to which in some respect the English would be heirs, also seemed to engender an uncomfortable permissiveness in everyday private life. Venice, writes Bouwsma, 'became a purveyor of pleasures to the upper classes of Europe, the gaudiest stop on the Grand Tour.' Liberty and pleasure: it had to be decided whether in some respects or in some way these were compatible,[3] and it has to be concluded that in the Georgian ideal of a liberal education they were not. The connection of licence with liberal caused the Georgians no end of difficulty and confusion, producing an ambivalence that penetrated deeply into the culture, as will be apparent in my later discussion. Their incompatibility in large measure accounts for the reaction that met the publication of Chesterfield's *Letters* in the 1770s. Far too often spoken of as a representative or ideal-type Georgian polite figure, Chesterfield just as much represents the other side of those ideals. He was discoursing on the worldly part of the ideal of a liberal education, which required education to be, as more than

[1] Vicesimus Knox, *Liberal Education*, 11th ed., II (London, 1795), 129.
[2] William Blackstone, *Commentaries on the Laws of England*, I (Oxford, 1765), 37.
[3] William Bouwsma, 'Venice and the Political Education of Europe', in *Renaissance Venice*, ed. J. R. Hale (London, 1973), 461–2.

one commentator of the period said, 'a rehearsal of life'. Very well, then: life, the world, is vicious. Unfortunately, dissimulation and self-seeking are part of it, and one must learn to live under those conditions. Chesterfield caught the ambivalence within Georgian polite education. His own greatest vice was to reveal unequivocably how easily civilized behaviour could be reduced to the lowest common denominator. The public that read his posthumous writings neither applauded his candour nor forgave him for disclosing a cultural secret.

4

London

IT WAS because of London in particular that the idea of the independent man with a liberal education took solid hold, for London in the eighteenth century was able to provide precisely the kind of emancipating social conditions presupposed by the idea. Without London, and without the extraordinary, revolutionary urban consciousness that formed in the course of the early eighteenth century, it is difficult to see how Georgian conceptions of liberal education could have either spread or flourished.

The centre of a far-flung commercial empire, the governing and administrative heart of the kingdom, London in the eighteenth century emerged as the largest and perhaps most important capital in Europe. According to all demographic estimates, London surpassed Paris for the first time in 1700. Its extraordinary population growth was mainly the consequence of migration from other parts of the kingdom, for London itself was unhealthy, and the infant mortality rate during several decades was calamitous. London provided a market for farming, light industry, for craftsmen who lived in the surrounding and interpenetrating countryside. The magnates and gentry and financiers had town houses in London, employed large numbers of servants, gardeners, and decorators, and engaged the services of tutors, attorneys, and builders. Portrait painters came to London to make their fortunes. Purveyors of both English and Italian forms of opera established themselves in various parts of the bursting city. Theatres and fashionable pleasure gardens, to which members of all classes came (for different reasons), contributed to the life and excitement of the metropolis. It was in the eighteenth century that the Englishman, especially the

Londoner, became conscious of the fact that he was a city-dweller. In fact, 'civilization', when the word made its late historical appearance, was associated with the phenomenon of urban growth.[1]

To be sure, London had attracted the rural gentry before. They came in large numbers as early as the reigns of James I and Charles I to be nearer the royal court and Parliament, to consult lawyers, to drive coaches (newly introduced) through Hyde Park (which had not been a parade ground before) in the hope of being seen. They came, as Ben Jonson said, to turn four or five acres of their best land into two or three trunks of apparel.[2] They came for the London Season; in fact, they invented the Season, and most went home afterwards, although a few always stayed. It was the very beginnings of a trend, but just the beginnings. And after the economic retrenchment of the 1630s, necessitated by the precarious financial situation of the crown, London lost much of its attraction. Important segments of the gentry and peerage stayed away in anger and disappointment.[3] The rediscovery of London came much later in the seventeenth century, but it was the metropolis rather than the court that gained. After the civil war London as a place or city became separate in idea from the royal court. It was only then that the Londoner sharply, suddenly, realized that he was a city-dweller, that it was unique to be a city-dweller; and not until the late seventeenth century, when the financial and banking revolution occurred, did London set the example of fashion and high living for other English cities and towns.

In the Elizabethan period the rural gentry were satisfied with their regional capitals and occasionally in Stuart times built houses there. They spoke the language of the province and did not look to London for the latest gossip, fashions, or excitement. The ablest men of the towns were content to stay there and contribute their energies to the life of the neighbourhood.[4] It

[1] Lefebvre, 59–60.
[2] F. J. Fisher, 'The Development of London as a Centre of Conspicuous Consumption', in *Transactions of the Royal Historical Society*, 4th ser., XXX (1948), 48.
[3] Lawrence Stone, *The Crisis of the Aristocracy, 1558–1641* (Oxford, 1965), 502.
[4] W. G. Hoskins, 'An Elizabethan Provincial Town: Leicester', in *Studies in Social History*, ed. J. H. Plumb (London, 1955), 35, 38.

was in the 1690s that London began to separate itself culturally from the rest of the kingdom. An invidious distinction was drawn between province and capital. All the areas outside London were indiscriminately called by the snide epithet 'Hampshire'. Norwich, the second city of the kingdom in the late seventeenth century, took the hint and copied the capital. In the course of the eighteenth century its old Cockney Lane was renamed 'London Street', and one of its attractive, much-frequented walks was called the 'Mall of Norwich'.[1]

To appreciate London's contributions to the history of culture (and hence to the history of a liberal education), to understand the meaning of urbanity or the sense of the superiority of city life—the belief that being civilized is best achieved in a city— we must appreciate certain primary aspects of the history of the capital. Foremost among these is the fact that England had never been, like Italy, a country of cities and city-states, with traditions of independent government and republican principles. This explains why Renaissance civic humanism lost much of its force and meaning when it transferred to England. A 'city' in England was a diocesan seat possessing a splendid cathedral, or it was a commercial or legal entity, a collection of guilds or a corporation. The peace of a cathedral close, the limited business of small market towns and smaller villages: these meant more in the consciousness of everyday life than did cities. The Englishman may have had his coat of arms (bogus or legitimate) engraved on his plate, painted above his door or on his carriage, or he may have been depicted with his horses and dogs; but he did not hold his city in his hands as did the saints of Italy, who today look at us from the paintings and frescoes of the Siena school.

Before urban consciousness could establish itself on a new basis, incorporating ideas of cosmopolitanism and sophistica-

---

[1] Penelope Corfield, 'A Provincial Capital in the Late Seventeenth Century: The Case of Norwich', in *Crisis and Order in English Towns, 1500–1700*, eds. Peter Clark and Paul Slack (London, 1972), 289, 290, 293. My colleague Irwin Scheiner informs me that he notices a similar separation of capital from province in Japan at about the same time as in England. From the end of the seventeenth century Edo developed an urban identity based on its mercantile and artistic achievements which was distinct from prevailing court, samurai, or folk cultures.

tion, especially the idea that the city-dweller—particularly the man who lives in a great capital—is in touch with the highest *international* achievements in art, literature, and culture, London had to decisively reject the influence of the English court. This development occurred first in the middle of the seventeenth century but was not fully realized until the next century. We can follow its route by pausing for a moment over the history of the civic pageant or municipal 'show' of the early modern period. In the age of Elizabeth, London pageants were effectively dominated by the crown. While representatives of City guild interests were certainly participants, and important participants, in the great street parades of the period, national not civic concerns were pre-eminent. Allegories and other *tableaux vivants* celebrated the virtues of a dynasty threatened with enemies foreign and domestic, of a queen who might die without issue. Increasingly in the seventeenth century, however, the personal authority of the monarch declined for well-known political reasons, and as it did, almost in reciprocal fashion the civic pageant came more and more to reflect London interests, especially its commercial and mercantile activities. The spectacular royal entry pageants of Queen Elizabeth, announcing her apotheosis as Deborah, or Peace, or the Fairy Queen, wildly exalting her singular religious and even mystical powers, came to an end in the reigns of her immediate successors. The Lord Mayor accompanied by the liveried companies of London replaced the sovereign beneath the marvellous triumphal arches. The court, no longer dominating London symbolically, retreated from street to palace. Pageants staged outdoors for city crowds were abandoned in favour of masques performed indoors for the courtly few.[1] London was now free to create an urban consciousness based not only upon its long-standing civic guildism but also upon a developing sense of the inherent superiority of city life.

While the decline of royal influence was necessary for the creation of a special urban identity, it was not sufficient to produce the cosmopolitanism and the worldliness, the urbane cultural pride of Georgian London. Before this could be achieved, London had to improve its international and economic position.

[1] See David M. Bergeron, *English Civic Pageantry 1558–1642* (London, 1971).

This occurred first in the 1690s, the decade that truly marks a watershed in London's history. In the period following, Louis XIV was defeated on the continent, thus stimulating national pride; the Englishman on tour abroad with money to burn became a familiar sight; and an imperial position was obtained and extended. At the turn of the century that important man of letters, Joseph Addison, holding forth in Button's, could call himself a 'Citizen of the World', and mean thereby that London was a microcosm of Europe, a place where different nationalities could gather to create a capital of culture, toleration, and enterprise.

London cosmopolitanism in a narrow sense was not possible until Addison's time, for it was only at the turn of the century that conspicuous numbers of foreign merchants settled in London to live and work. While there had always been foreign communities resident in London, they were small. The old Hanse had representatives in London as early as the eleventh century, but their trading rights were formally abrogated in 1552. A handful of Ragusans were also to be found in London, and one such family even owned land in Kent and Sussex. In the sixteenth century Italian merchants were the most important London exporters, controlling the trade in kerseys, worsteds, linens, and fustians, and a number of them were later absorbed into English society. But at their highpoint in the mid sixteenth century, Ragusans and Italians together numbered no more than 26, hardly a size to lend to London the tone of a great international capital.[1]

Before the eighteenth century the men who boasted most of the cultural superiority of London were the wits at the royal court, a group separate and distinct from the metropolis. But after the 1690s the boast of London's greatness was taken up by new groups of men, by writers, journalists, critics, intellectuals, and polemicists whose lives were led not at court but in the city itself. London was emerging as a special place requiring a special sort of engagement and a different set of values. Throughout the eighteenth century the feeling that life in London imposed unique requirements on its inhabitants continued. From one

[1] G. D. Ramsay, 'The Undoing of the Italian Mercantile Colony in Sixteenth-Century London', in *Textile History and Economic History*, eds. N. B. Harte and K. G. Ponting (Manchester, 1973), 22–49.

end of the century to another the imaginative writers and novelists and architects were at work defining and elaborating the special characteristics of London and at the same time exploring their own responses to it. Much of the exploration was, to begin with, still convention, echoes of the antagonism between town and country that goes back at least to Horace and Virgil, variations on inherited pastoral themes and on the benefits of retirement and return to the land, as if the full meaning of city life had not yet become apparent. Hence the desire to blur the distinction between town and country, which we also find in London's history, in Georgian town planning, where parks, gardens, and open spaces were arranged to achieve harmony between nature and urban life. Increasingly, London was accepted on its own terms, and the city became the primary place of residence for millions of Englishmen and an indispensable part of their self-conception and identity.

There is an important difference in the way Georgian writers and journalists viewed London and the way it was seen later. By and large, the Georgians responded enthusiastically to London. Living in London, despite the predators and parasites, the jobocrats and beggars, the social climbers and drunks, the great emergent Vanity Fair (Thackeray's, not Bunyan's) was a positive experience, stimulating, challenging, broadening. Foreigners of all kinds continued to crowd into London, spreading into Soho as they had once spread into the City and adding their colour to it. London was a source of constant excitement and novelty. Talent flowed to it like the Thames from the nether reaches of the country. The Tweed was another of its tributaries. Although the cry for escape from London is continuous throughout the eighteenth century, the dominant impression that we are left with is that London was fresh, new, engaging, even if dangerous and the seat of affectation.

Georgian writers on education were unable to ignore the ramifications of urban life for the meaning of a liberal education. London was a formidable challenge to the whole notion of education for moral conduct in everyday life. Addison set the pace for one form of response by directly confronting the challenge. Let education move out of the usual formal institutions or homes, he said, 'out of closets and libraries, schools and colleges, to dwell in clubs and assemblies, at tea-tables, and in coffee-houses.'[1] When Georgian authors wrote about liberal education, they wrote about urbanity, about the values required to live in a cosmopolitan, free-wheeling, and demanding environment. They thought about the need for sophistication in coping with a complicated society and about manners and worldliness. They gave little thought to the meaning of civic (or civil) responsibility, a tradition that arrived by another route and was related to the politics of the period, as Pocock and others have shown.[2] For the Georgians the purpose of a liberal education always referred back in some way to the experience of living in the brave new world of London that had so many wonders in it.

The place where the ends of a liberal education were the most appreciated and in fact encouraged, the epitome of urbanity and sociability, the home of civilization—unquestionably this was London. But London also possessed every temptation to vice and corruption—like Venice, exemplified the paradox of liberty and licence. When London reached the nineteenth century, its wonders began to pall and fade, to disturb and frighten. The voices raised against it were Cobbett's and De Quincey's. The city that Dr. Johnson loved became Shelley's, a place something like hell. The contradictions that had always been part of London's history were viewed less complacently, and there was no longer any Georgian optimism present to cause men to avert their eyes.[3]

Education moved back from the clubs, salons, closets, and coffee-houses of London to the traditional centres of instruction. London's presence had become a handicap, not an advantage, in

[1] *Spectator*, Number 10.
[2] E.g., J. G. A. Pocock, 'Virtue and Commerce in the Eighteenth Century', in *The Journal of Interdisciplinary Studies*, III (Summer, 1972), 119–34.
[3] The relationship of an intellectual class or intelligentsia to the emergence of a capital as both cause and consequence is a fascinating topic. Parallels can be drawn between European capitals, although all historical parallels have their limits. Wolfgang Sauer, in a stimulating article, has noticed how the rise to independent or semi-independent status of a twentieth-century German intelligentsia has also meant the rise of a 'Berlin culture', a culture (taking the term rather more broadly than I use it) of the capital, which Berlin, unlike London or Paris, had not been. Wolfgang Sauer, 'Weimar Culture: Experiments in Modernism', in *Social Research*, 39 (Summer, 1972), 276.

education. It was better to raise young men in towns and country places far removed from London. Schools like Charterhouse that had once been in the country but had become enveloped by spreading London changed their location. Oxford and Cambridge dons began to bestir themselves, to look less longingly on the attractions of the capital, and to assert a new discipline over undergraduates. When University College was established in the late 1820s, opponents were not slow to point out the dangers to discipline the London environment created. Partly, of course, they wanted an excuse to attack the first experiment in secular higher education in England. But no such excuse was required a few years later when a respectable Anglican university college was established in the Strand. It could in all honesty be said that a problem was indeed presented by the proximity of King's College to the Haymarket theatres, known to be frequented by ladies of easy virtue. The only answer was for 'Minerva by gaslight' to trust to the established religion. If we require a symbol for the rejection of London by the foremost educational institutions, it came in the second quarter of the nineteenth century, when Oxford University diverted the Great Western Railway to the town of Didcot, some ten miles to the south, thus preventing the great capital from penetrating to the very doorsteps of the university.

5

Classics and Classical Education

A DISCUSSION of the social and cultural meaning of a particular theory of education is essential to understanding its use, but, of course, such a discussion does not tell us why a particular group of subjects is chosen as the principal means of applying the theory. It does not explain why one curriculum is chosen in preference to another, nor does it describe the linkage between subject and theory. If the cultural goal in the Georgian period was civility, we have still to understand how it was conceived in purely educational language.

In some respects the answer is simpler than we may desire. It is also familiar. In eighteenth-century England a liberal education was basically literary. It was book learning: this meant both training in language, to include foreign and especially classical languages, and works of literature written in those languages. We must not mistakenly think (as is all too common) that this was an excessively restricted education. In theory, at least, and to some extent in practice, the study of classical languages introduced the student to an enormous range of learning: poetry, drama, biography, history, political theory, geography, ethnography, philosophy, logic, ethics, rhetoric, architecture. Classical education drew from all creative periods, from Hesiod to the Byzantine Empire to Christian Europe, from Italian Renaissance scholarship, Dutch humanism, French neoclassicism. Science, at least scientific method and thought, biological classification, theories of motion, astronomy, physiology were, of course, also part of the ancient inheritance, transmitted, if piecemeal, over the centuries. In the seventeenth century Greek corpuscularism found its way into Europe through Epicurus, himself having drawn on Democritus and

Leucippus. Besides classical literature and texts, modern writing in the vernacular languages of Europe showed up on lists of liberal topics and authors. Shakespeare and Milton, Bunyan and Spenser were naturally known and read as part of the national literature, but even foreigners were represented: thinkers from France like Boileau, Pascal, Talleyrand, and Montaigne; architects like Perrault; and philosophers from the Low Countries like Vossius.

The eighteenth century was therefore heir to virtually all of the writings of classical antiquity that had become so central to the culture and thought of western civilization. This was as true, or nearly as true, of Greek literature as Latin. It is certainly not possible to claim that the classical corpus received and used by Englishmen or Scotsmen of the late seventeenth and eighteenth centuries was fundamentally Latin or Roman and not Hellenic, that the age was Augustan and not Attic. Classical Greek authors, Hellenistic Greek authors, early Christian Greek authors, and Byzantine Greek authors were known and read. Famous translations were made: Thucydides by Hobbes, Homer, of course, by diverse hands. A serious school of neoplatonic studies appeared at Cambridge in the mid seventeenth century, although it never gained a lasting place in the curriculum. Polybius had an important influence on eighteenth-century constitutional theory. Isocrates, Pindar, and the Greek tragedians were known. A private tutor compiled a list in 1710, which he made public in 1730, of Greek authors recommended for the use of students. His list included Xenophon, Lucian, Theophrastus, Dionysius, Demosthenes, Hesiod, Theocritus, Homer, Sophocles, Euripides, Thucydides, and Diogenes Laertius.[1] The list of Greek authors which Augustan scholars and writers encountered and recommended for general reading is long and impressive.

Greek and Latin literature, encompassing virtually all fields of scholarship and science, comprised the tradition received over the centuries. But this by no means recounts the whole story. For while classical languages and classical learning constituted in the broadest sense the educational heritage of England and Europe, there were important shifts in emphasis and purpose within that heritage. The uses to which classical learning was

---

[1] Waterland, 18–31.

put were never constant. By the beginning of the eighteenth century distinct trends were already in operation that set the Georgian period apart from preceding centuries and directly affected the character and function of liberal instruction.

To understand the departures within the received classical inheritance, it is necessary for a moment to review certain aspects of the earlier history of classical education in England. For a time in the earliest sixteenth century it appeared that the new learning associated with the Italian Renaissance would make a significant impact on the forms of English education. The *studia humanitatis* has been brought across the Channel from Italy, principally in connection with the ideal of the statesman, and made a good start in the reign of Henry VIII, but it did not succeed in taking hold in any of the traditional educational institutions. Reasons of State reduced the new learning to a subordinate position and left it largely in the hands of private tutors. English Renaissance humanism was the possession of a few exceptional men and did not exercise any appreciable or lasting influence on either the grammar schools or the ancient universities.[1]

In the seventeenth century the new learning can still be encountered in England, and from the standpoint of the history of modern experimental science the century is a brilliant one; but, as in the preceding era, the new learning, whether 'humane' or scientific, failed to make a major impact on the structure of secondary and university education. Within the universities the tradition of instruction and study was still emphatically scholastic; famous classical authors, while they inspired the curriculum (although more indirectly than directly), did not necessarily occupy a central position in the official studies. Thus one graduate of Cambridge recalled his work in 1618 as 'Seton's Logic . . . and part of Keckerman's and Molineus. Of ethics, or moral philosophy . . . Gellius and part of Pickolomineus; of physics, part of Magirus; and of history, part of Florus. . . . [A]lso I perused . . . Gellius' Attic Nights, and part of Macrobius' Saturnals.'[2]

---

[1] Kenneth Charlton, *Education in Renaissance England* (London, 1965), 130–68.

[2] Costello, 41.

It is not until the late seventeenth century or the beginning of the eighteenth century that we actually encounter in England the teaching of classical languages and literature for the express purpose of promoting 'humane learning'. The phrase itself had been used as early as the beginning of the seventeenth century but not to indicate the supreme position that specific classical authors occupied in the educational curriculum or the admiration they inspired in learned Europeans. The famous men of antiquity had not been studied because they were 'classics' or because they had written masterpieces with which every man of culture and taste had to be familiar, but because their writings formed the starting point for learning method, for undertaking studies in logic, ethics, and theology. The subjects had always been more important than the 'authorities.'

In 1700 Jean Le Clerc's *Parrhasiana* was translated, making available in English what had already been available in French, thus offering to Englishmen a new equation, that of classical literature with 'humane learning'.[1] From that moment on, humane learning came specifically to mean the direct study of the most renowned classical texts, and especially those authors who were literary figures. The new emphasis had a profound and unfortunate impact on the history of English science. The educated community of England divided into two groups (as did the educated community of France), the Ancients or the classicists, and the Moderns or the scientists. Science, which had been one of the truly exciting intellectual activities of the second half of the seventeenth century, was now attacked by the proponents of classical education as insufficiently polite or civilized. Members of the Royal Society, the official home of institutional science, were especially sensitive to the charge because their antagonists appeared to be speaking in the name of the higher taste and refinement. The Royal Society subsequently became concerned with making science respectable in social terms. '[A]ll the various manners of *Education*, will remain undisturb'd,' wrote its historian and principal apologist.[2]

[1] James William Johnson, *The Formation of English Neo-Classical Thought* (Princeton, 1967), 8–9.

[2] Quoted in Charles Webster, 'Science and the Challenge to the Scholastic Curriculum, 1640–1660', in *The Changing Curriculum*, History of Education Society (London, 1971), 33–4.

This meant divorcing it to a large extent from the servile arts, from earlier useful projects like the development of navigational instruments and steam power.[1] Thus began a new justification for the study of science, at least by those anxious to be thought fashionable and correct, that it was, like classical education, a branch of humane or polite learning. It was said of chemistry, the pre-eminent eighteenth-century science, that its study accomplished precisely the same ends of liberal instruction as classical languages. One author claimed that the study of chemistry enlarged the mind and softened manners.[2]

The fundamental reason why Le Clerc's humanist definition of classical learning was adopted and the reason for its extra-ordinary later influence is precisely because of the ease with which it suited the ends of a liberal education. As the entire purpose of liberal education was to lubricate interpersonal relations and to promote public affairs, nothing could be more educationally worthwhile than studying those classical texts that bore directly on the conduct of everyday life. The proper study of mankind was man. In response to this directive, irresistible in the changing cultural circumstances of Georgian England, Englishmen turned to the famous works of rhetoric and elocu-tion, to the writings of historians and biographers that offered abundant examples of virtuous behaviour, honourable conduct, civic patriotism, noble self-sacrifice, and stoic self-restraint. They turned as well to the 'stylish' authors, to those classical writers who could provide models for exactly the kind of public image and appearance required in an outgoing, sociable age.

These were the basic reasons for the remarkable ascendancy of classical authors and ideas in the eighteenth century. There were also related secondary reasons. Ancient literature was a record of the progress of civilization upward from barbarism and out of gothic night. The historic connection between Christianity and the Latin language, the ethical doctrines that had made their way from Rome to Christianity, and the prag-matic characteristics of Roman civilization all recommended the study of classics to Englishmen, as did the generalizing

[1] Margaret 'Espinasse, 'The Decline and Fall of Restoration Science', in *Past and Present*, 14 (November, 1958), 71–89.

[2] A. D. Godley, *Oxford in the Eighteenth Century* (London and New York, 1908), 66.

nature of classical thought, of obvious use to an age which also wished to think in universal terms.

It is, of course, evident that to some extent the interests of an educated person in classical learning depended upon his occupational concerns. It goes without saying that a Restoration or Georgian poet would select those texts which provided him with either a subject or a form essential to his task, that an historian would be interested in historical or constitutional questions, a philosopher in the corpus of ancient philosophical writing, teachers of elocution would be interested in the rhetorical writers and logicians, and so on. Choices made in this way could vary not only from poet to historian, but also from poet to poet, depending upon whether he was interested in pastoral, lyric, epic, or elegiac poetry, or verse drama.

But choices also depended on factors other than taste or preference, and it is necessary to bear in mind the organization for teaching in Georgian England. The variations in recommended readings so prevalent in the period can be called a by-product of the decentralization of education in the eighteenth century. The State was not interested in 'national education'—indeed, the idea had not yet occurred. The Church, which was interested in education, because of its continuing rivalry with Dissent, still did not have a firm policy and left the direction of studies to local or personal initiative, or to the forces of the market. The demand for education and the demand for particular levels of education varied radically from period to period and from group to group, depending upon social and economic circumstances, occupational distributions, and cultural values. Countless persons, lay as well as clerical, opened schools, tried out various educational experiments and programmes in an effort to retain a fickle or uncertain clientele. And home tuition, where adjustments in curricula could be made quickly and easily according to the learning ability of the pupil, certainly remained one of the most important means of elementary and secondary education throughout the eighteenth century.

From an institutional point of view, the result was a vigorous but often short-lived collection of educational arrangements, institutions that had little to do with one another. Each schoolmaster or teacher or tutor felt it incumbent upon himself to make his own selection of texts and to justify his choice by appropriate advertizing. The number of authors recommended as suitable for a liberal education multiplied in the eighteenth century. Not every pupil read the same works nor did the same amount of reading, nor did he spend the same number of years in school. This being the case, schoolmasters did not, on the whole, worry about continuity in studies from one place of education to another, either from the home to the school, from one school to another, or from school to university. The historical consequence of this pattern is clear. At every stage of his educational career, the pupil could expect to repeat what he already knew without anyone caring what he had already been taught. Masters, regarding other masters as rivals rather than co-operators in the task of general education, did not value the instruction offered by their competitors and were reluctant to believe that pupils in their charge had received adequate teaching elsewhere. From the standpoint of medieval scholasticism, repeating lessons is the only way to learn; but at some point it is self-defeating. It is an inevitable conclusion that the eighteenth-century school pupil and university student were far too often bored.

Greek authors were widely known and cited, but it is true that Latin was the essential language as far as the Georgian grammar schools were concerned. Many grammar schools were in fact known by the designation 'Latin schools', and Greek was studied through the use of Latin grammars. In the universities, classical learning was mainly centred in the colleges, although it did not receive equal emphasis in all of them. The university curriculum, rapidly decaying, was essentially scholastic —that is, logic was the backbone of the archaic examination system.

In the second half of the eighteenth century important changes occurred. In the schools Greek authors received more attention, and the language itself was studied with the assistance of new, non-Latin grammars, although this was not true of Eton. The preliminary steps were being taken that would ultimately produce the nineteenth-century emphasis on Greek history, political thought, and philosophy. At the same time, a shift towards the study of ancient civilization itself took place with great enthusiasm and excitement. Classical studies were boosted still more by the development of archaeology and the serious beginnings of comparative philology. The discovery of vases and vase paintings in Greece and Southern Italy, the subsequent excavations at Herculaneum and elsewhere added a first-hand dimension to classical studies and opened up another dazzling chapter in painting and architecture. In one sense, it is possible to say that the archaeological discoveries of the late eighteenth century were simply another phase of the century-old desire in England to get close to the original sources of Greek civilization. But in another sense, the feeling of radical discovery that permeates the entire later period, whether we call it the age of neoclassicism or the Hellenic revival, is an unmistakable indicator of an entirely new texture of thought. The more systematic and scholarly the researches into the history of ancient civilization became and the more that was published on the complexities of the Mediterranean world, the less was it possible to make past experience analogous to the present. To be sure, the search for parallels continued and has perhaps never ceased. But the real value of classical learning had to be justified on other grounds, on its use as an intellectual tool and as an instrument for forming the mind. When this happened, classics ceased to be humane learning and became, ironically, science. This development, however, is part of the later history of a liberal education and must be discussed in an appropriate context.

For our present purposes, there is one final connection between Georgian culture, liberal education, and the classical inheritance that requires examination, and that is the theory of artistic creativity that forms part of the Greek doctrine of imitation. The importance of this doctrine to the liberally-educated gentlemen of the illustrious reign of the Georges should not be overlooked. Since eighteenth-century liberal education was literary, and since the purpose of liberal education was social, what was needed as part of the educational process was a theory or explanation of the function of literature, or the relationship of literature to life. This the mimetic doctrine was able to provide.

The definition usually employed was Aristotle's: imitation was a representation of ultimate truth. Universal reality, ideal reality, as opposed to private or personal experience, had to provide the model for artistic enterprise, whether visual or literary. Virtually every European artist or poet or writer on aesthetics concerned with the meaning or function of art returned to this fundamental definition and repeated it, from the Renaissance onwards, citing the authority of the great Peripatetic. Over the centuries, however, Aristotle's meaning was distorted, its central point lost, and by the time the doctrine attributed to him reached the waiting Georgians, it had been completely twisted out of shape. The Georgians had not received Aristotle so much as Plato, although transmitted via Horace. As in general eighteenth-century Englishmen did not know their Plato well, Horace served agreeably in his absence. In general, Georgian authors did not mind using the corrupted Aristotelian text, for the impure version of mimesis was actually better suited to their purpose, and they applied it eagerly to the theory of liberal education already in the process of formation.

Aristotle carefully distinguished between representation and reality. The two were not synonymous. The function of art was not to duplicate reality—that is, life—nor even to approximate it. The object was to represent ultimate reality in such a way as to provide the observer with materials for pleasurable contemplation—that is, for the joy of understanding. Aristotle called this a cathartic experience, by which he meant a growing understanding or insight into the meaning of tragic existence. By no means did he wish to convey the conclusion that the function of art was merely the imitation of an action, or somehow a copy of life. In the Platonic-Horatian tradition, however, the careful Aristotelian distinction between the purpose of art and the reality of ultimate experience was thoroughly demolished. Art and reality were fused together, provided with mutually binding responsibilities. A particular kind of experience, which we can call art or poetry or literature, was substituted for another, to which we give the name life or reality or ultimate experience. The result of this metonym was a very different conclusion from the one Aristotle had reached. The function of art was not catharsis or pleasurable contemplation. It was not a special awareness of the meaning of existence generated from within a particular work of art. Since art and life were interchangeable for Plato and Horace, the function of art was no less than the establishment of ideal modes of conduct, of making literature a vehicle for moral precepts, of philosophy teaching by example. As Johnson seemed to tell Boswell, catharsis was a kind of poetical diuretic by which impurities were 'purged', that is, expelled from the emotions; or to put it more politely, it was the process by which the passions were either chastened or refined.[1]

The Platonic metonym, confusing art with life and carried forward into the eighteenth century by the tradition of Roman rhetoric, was precisely what the Georgians in their pursuit of civility, moral improvement, and human happiness wanted. Plato's theory of the purpose of literature was easily turned into a didactic theory of education as Aristotle's mimesis could never be. Literature, painting, and poetry were solidly connected to proper manners, criticism to moral lessons, rhetoric to right conduct, taste to virtue. 'The chief end [of literature] seems to have been instruction,' wrote Sir William Temple towards the end of the seventeenth century, repeating the doctrine of mimesis as he understood it, 'and under the disguise of fables, or the pleasure of a story, to show the beauties and the rewards of virtue, the difformities [*sic.*] and misfortunes or punishment of vice, by examples of both to encourage one, and deter men from the other; to reform ill customs, correct ill manners, and moderate all violent passions.'[2] Catharsis or the joy of insight into a portion of the human experience shifted to social utility as the central meaning of imitation. The tragic theatre declined and satire flourished, exactly as Augustan and Georgian humanism required. Given the cultural purposes of the age, there could be no other outcome.

[1] Dominique Secretan, *Classicism* (London, 1973), 55–6.
[2] John D. Boyd, S.J., *The Function of Mimesis and Its Decline* (Cambridge, Mass., 1968), 150. I have profited substantially from this illuminating book.

6

'Taste'

A STIMULATING pioneering work in the sociology of culture establishes a direct correlation between changes in literary forms and changes in the social structure of Georgian England.[1] But we cannot speak now with the same assurance about the social class origins of particular artistic activity. The history of literary preference in the eighteenth century is not primarily a history of the rise of the middle classes. But although no very certain or satisfactory class interpretations of literary and artistic choice are possible, there can be no doubt that alterations in the relationship of groups to one another must be considered in establishing the meaning of a liberal education in the Hanoverian period. The interpenetration of classes and groups in eighteenth-century London does help explain the persistence of one particular cultural idea that became closely associated with the goals of a liberal education: 'Taste' (in the singular).

'Taste', writes the author of a celebrated work in the history of ideas, 'can be found throughout the Italian and French 17th centuries as a term, but it becomes the subject of elaborate theorizing only in the early 18th century.'[2] In England the idea of Taste was a cultural inheritance that can be called Augustan—that is, it was connected to the poetry and philosophical writing of the late seventeenth century. To Shaftesbury, reacting to the material philosophy of his tutor Locke, Taste was Platonic, abstract, *a priori*, pre-existing. Taste belonged to the same intellectual level of classification as Nature or Reason, and in

[1] Leo Lowenthal, *Literature, Popular Culture, and Society* (Palo Alto, California, 1968, first issued 1961). See also Diana Spearman, *The Novel and Society* (London, 1966), for a counter view.

[2] René Wellek, *A History of Modern Criticism*, I (New Haven, 1955), 24.

the early eighteenth century all three were closely related. The latter two were in fact often equivalent. To follow the rules of one was *ipso facto* to follow the rules of the other; and either one of them, Nature or Reason, could be a guide for Taste.

By the middle of the eighteenth century, as the patronage system in the arts began to decline in importance, it could no longer be assumed that the patron and the artist, writer or composer, held shared assumptions. The means for determining what Taste was and how it was to be acquired underwent a corresponding change. Nature, the support of Taste, became less abstract, less an objective determinant of what was considered correct, and more commonly a part of everyday experience. To a large extent, this new sense of Nature was furthered by the philosophy of induction and scientific empiricism. The result was a concept of Taste far more relative than it had been in the idealist writings of Shaftesbury. Since everyday experience in a society of rapid urban transformation was various and to a great extent chaotic, a subjective dimension began to appear in the definition of Taste and to threaten it with its plural form. The debates over the Eclectic Style are adequate illustrations of the division of feeling on the matter. For some artists 'eclectic' was a bad word, the rejection of a standard, and for others it indicated freedom without altogether abandoning past examples. Lord Kames was worried that a Saracen's head on a pub sign would be valued as much as the best 'tablature of Raphael',[1] as well he might be, when a thinker of another tradition was about to change the comparison to 'push-pin and poetry'. In retrospect we can see that the Eclectic Style was a clear and direct response to an opening consumer market.

If Taste cannot be decided in advance, if cultural styles compete and yet the artist still believes in the idea of a standard that ought to dominate the market, one of two alternatives has to be recognized: either the subjective inclinations of the artist must be acknowledged by the buying public, or subjective responses must be subordinated by the artist himself to a clearly defined, or at least acceptable, standard. At the very minimum, the artist has to modify his position.

The first alternative, characteristic of the French avant garde

---

[1] Quoted in Joan Pittock, *The Ascendancy of Taste* (London, 1973), 52.

movement of the last one hundred years, demands the most of the public. The author makes no attempt to please his readers, he cares (or claims he does) more about creating than communicating, and his attitude towards the public is contemptuous. Art becomes esoteric and threatens to become private. Not that all artists in all times have been either perfectly comprehensible or accommodating to the wishes of their patrons. The change was rather in the attitude of the artist towards his public and the length to which he was willing to go to assert his independence. But Georgian artists stopped far short of the avant garde idea, for it was historically too much to ask of men who were just emerging from the ascendancy of the patron. It was too much to ask of a public that may have been uncertain of its own taste but still felt comfortable surrounded by the visible signs of a great artistic tradition from which it did not care to be emancipated (if that is the word).

The second alternative, which allowed numerous variations, was the one adopted by the middle of the eighteenth century. The desire to have a standard of some kind was retained as a general control over artistic production, but the attempt to carry out this desire resulted in a cultural compromise with widespread ramifications and a fundamental departure from the position taken by intellectuals of the preceding century.

In the late seventeenth century artists and aestheticians had depended upon convention, upon what were called rules of art, and upon platonic influences to decide the characteristics of Taste. Small, clearly perceived audiences made the task easier. But the turn to a wider and anonymous audience of mixed social composition, literary attainment, and aesthetic experience rendered the customary modes of determining excellence unsatisfactory. Artists experimented with their publics by self-consciously trying to touch their emotions, and the potential response of the public became a central concern in the creation of works of art. But as this seemed to assign too much authority to what might after all turn out to be mere feckless taste, artists sought additional grounds for establishing canons of discrimination. They turned to psychology. Equating their audiences with human nature in the abstract, they deduced working principles of aesthetic composition from what were presumed to be general psychological traits or universal qualities of human nature.

Both eighteenth-century neoclassicism and moral philosophy encouraged this decision. Furthermore, applying the same assumptions about human nature to themselves, they analysed their own minds as a likely indication of audience response.[1] The upshot of these developments was that the word Taste was loosened in application, as were its companion words. 'Nature', for example, descended to 'natural', and natural was used to describe personal and not necessarily abstract or hypothetical feelings and emotions as had been the earlier case. Impressions were accorded a much greater role in assessing the worth of a particular work of art, but there followed a continual attempt in aesthetic theory to elevate impressions to scientific or universal status, an attempt in keeping with what remained a classicizing tradition.

Two consequences ultimately followed from these important changes. The author or artist acquired a new role as an astute observer of the world around him,[2] even a reputation as a man of affairs, and in his own estimation he rose in importance, having found objective reasons for doing as he liked.

In the second half of the eighteenth century a new vocabulary of emotional response appeared to express both the loosening of previous rules of artistic creativity and the desire to retain some kind of ultimate control over the range of feelings likely to be released. Words like 'sublime', 'picturesque', 'sensibility', and 'sentiment' entered the language from various sources to establish the boundaries of emotional response. These became the subjects of common aesthetic discussion.

The new vocabulary or grammar of emotions can be assessed in two different yet related cultural ways, although each taken alone moves the significance of the change in a direction different from the other. The first way stresses the innovation, the introduction of a more emotional, less exclusively cerebral, mode of response and the departure from traditional canons of style. The second way stresses the strength of continuity, the hold of past values on changing ones, and the desire to restrict the range of

---

[1] For some useful remarks on the shifting philosophical foundations of aesthetic theory see James S. Malek, 'The Influence of Empirical Psychology on Aesthetic Discourse; Two Eighteenth Century Theories of Art', in *Enlightenment Essays*, I (Spring, 1970).

[2] Lowenthal, 78.

available choice. Here the emphasis is not so much on breaking away to explore new areas of personal experience as on the *fear* engendered by the thought of breaking away. If one of Mrs. Radcliffe's heroines in what we now regard as a perfectly conventional gothic setting (a deserted abbey in the middle of lonely woods, moonlight illuminating ruins, and the thrill of danger ever present) announces that the setting and the situation are 'sublime', she is controlling her fear rather than indulging her imagination. She is using a word that restricts her appreciation of her surrounding circumstances as much as it heightens it. The experience she undergoes has a second-hand quality. Here is a difference between the romantic response of a later period, the active search for the unknown and for personal experience, and the unravelling of the Augustan concept of Taste in the second half of the eighteenth century. Much the same analysis can be applied to 'picturesque', another key word. Here the dominant idea is the transformation of a setting or scene that is by traditional standards disconcerting—a blasted heath or loathsome mountains, hideous eruptions of the earth's normally reassuring surface—into a pleasing or normal or safe form like a picture, a scene that can be framed and hung on a wall. Dr. Johnson did precisely this when climbing in the highlands with Boswell. He took along a Claude glass, a hand-held convex mirror, in order to reduce the scenes around him by looking at the reflection instead of the actual scenery. This act restored the correct relationship between man and nature by diminishing the scale of grandeur. A picturesque experience is like a sublime one in being at one remove from the actual experience; it is a controlled response to the unfamiliar. It is fascinating how strongly in cultural terms the eighteenth century resisted such private experiences despite the awakening desire to have them. The sublime and the picturesque were used in later Georgian England to designate experiences that were regarded as essentially unnatural, unusual, strange, or monstrous—in any case, abnormal. The only way out of this difficulty for writers anxious to ennoble loneliness was to regard it as a special experience— that is, to admit that the sublime and the picturesque were different and not normal, but at the same time to deny that this was without value. Such was the road to the romantic future and the exhaltation of privacy and loneliness.

'Taste'

One of the most significant developments accompanying the revised notion of Taste, indeed essential to it, was the emergence of the critic. If there is no single standard of Taste, there must nevertheless be a means of discerning what is good or what is better. In the Restoration such a specialist was not required. The Augustan idea of Taste, which was expressed mainly through poetry, to include verse drama, was inspired directly by classical ideas of literary excellence reinforced by seventeenth-century French neoclassicism, an influence on the court of Charles II. Potential audience response was not a significant factor in determining the modes of communication. Taste was a matter of accepting beforehand certain inherited canons of style. Except perhaps for the popular playhouse of the seventeenth century, the audience for secular poetry was limited essentially to the households of the great. Once, however, audience appeal became a consideration in fashioning creative works, an intermediary seemed necessary, someone who could explain the value and importance of a particular work. This is the important thought behind Johnson's remark that Addison sought a national standard of judging. He meant Taste could no longer be formed by the fashionable court wits.

Gradually over the first fifty years of the eighteenth century the critic emerged to independent status in literary history. And with his emergence came the search for new methods of assessing literary and cultural merit, and for new standards appropriate to changing conditions. In the second half of the century the range of critical tools widened impressively: association psychology, historical scholarship, philology (constructed in the first instance on the models of chemistry), and, finally, archaeology. Interestingly enough, the antiquarian—or virtuoso, as he was called in the seventeenth century—returned by the end of the eighteenth century as a member of the Society of Dilettanti. Earlier in the eighteenth century he had been dismissed as largely inconsequential. His interests were regarded as peculiar, and no artist or scientist could take seriously his uncritical liking for marvels and taste for trivia,[1] especially as these appeared to have no connection with the study of man.

[1] The classic account of the antiquarian is of course Walter E. Houghton, Jr., 'The English Virtuoso in the Seventeenth Century', *Journal of the History of Ideas*, III, numbers 1 and 2 (1942).

By the end of the century the knowledge required of the critic had so expanded as to give a new value to antiquarian enthusiasms properly chastened.

Not only did the critic acquire independent status in the eighteenth century, but artists and writers of every kind also achieved the essential Georgian objective of independence. The changing concept of Taste, and the artist's reworked theory which allowed him to control it, accompanied changes in his actual social and economic position. The two were in fact interrelated. Beginning with Hogarth in painting, Dryden in poetry, and Addison in literature, artists had searched for an alternative to aristocratic patronage and dependence on the rich. They sought the kind of independence that would allow them greater freedom in the selection of subjects, themes, and styles. The solution to their problem lay in the emergence of a voracious consumer demand, as exemplified especially by the London market.

Certain aspects of that market existed in the previous century where there had been a demand for both secular and religious literature. But by the middle of the eighteenth century the market for artistic and luxury goods and services had widened enormously. The sensational growth in conspicuous expenditure throughout the eighteenth century provided new occupational and income opportunities for men of low, inferior, middling, or indifferent birth.[1] If the buyer could not afford a canvas, plentiful engravings existed in an age when masterpieces were copied in other media. The great designers of furniture published pattern books with their designs for the use of country craftsmen and spread their influence around the kingdom in this way. Playwrights, who doubled as actors, noticed new opportunities for advancement in the form of changing audiences. Surveying the crowded benches and boxes from the boards of West End theatres, their eyes took in the new kind of theatregoers packing the London playhouses: men and women of money in one section, the critics in their corner, the ruffians upstairs in the galleries. It has been intriguingly suggested that the boisterous, demanding audiences of the mid eighteenth-century theatre,

[1] Raymond Williams has identified the social origins of writers between 1630 and 1830 in *The Long Revolution* (London and New York, 1961), 230–45.

wanting to 'participate' in the action before them, forced play-wrights to experiment with dramatic forms in an effort to gain communication.[1] This is another example of market response.

Unquestionably the London market was central to the emancipation from patronage of select groups of authors and artists and a spur to the growth of service occupations. Un-questionably, too, the independence made possible by changing market conditions enhanced the importance of liberal education as a status indicator. As servile occupations were converted into liberal ones, as trades became professions, artists, writers, and professional men generally vigorously asserted their claims to independence.

We must avoid a certain determinist impression by making the changing position of these new groups appear absolutely dependent on the free market. Without London, artists and writers would not have achieved the independence they sought, nor would their ideology of artistic leadership have spread. But we must remember that it is quite possible that the formulation of certain canons of taste by artists preceded the emancipating economic conditions which they presuppose. Above all, we must not overlook or underplay the efforts made by artists to reach and organize the market, or even in certain ways—for example, subscription publishing, the use of booksellers, gallery exhibitions of paintings, and the formation of new associations, academies, and clubs—to create it. The greatest writers and artists surveyed the market and made rational decisions on the basis of it, but they neither set out to flatter the public nor to pander to it. They left that to the literary hacks and poetasters. The common theme that united men of varying political and social beliefs and even family origin was that in all matters of taste or judgement the opinion of the artist should prevail. By the beginning of the nineteenth century the social and economic position of the successful writer or artist was strong enough for him to recite the motto of independence with great assurance. 'Absolute independence is of all things most necessary to a public man, whether in politics or literature. To be useful to his king and country, he must not only be a free man, but he must stand

[1] J'nan Sellery, 'Language and Moral Intelligence in the Enlighten-ment: Fielding's Plays and Pope's Dunciad', in *Enlightenment Essays*, ibid., 19–20.

aloof from everything which can be represented or misrepresented as personal dependence.' Thus spoke Sir Walter Scott in vehement opposition to the proposal that less successful members of the self-employed intelligentsia be guaranteed £100 per annum by a crown-sponsored academy or writers' association.[1]

Changes in the idea of Taste are evidence of remarkable cultural changes generally. All literary historians and sociologists of literature have been inevitably drawn to them as indicators of profound developments in social relationships. Undoubtedly the importance of these developments will require further investigation, but their direct importance for the history of a liberal education can be summarized. By the end of the eighteenth century one important purpose of a liberal education was to produce critical standards of evaluation—or, as writers put it (borrowing from Locke who took the word from French writers), of 'judgement'—in all questions likely to affect personal conduct or social relations. Judgement was necessary because standards of value and morality were in danger of pulling away from familiar anchorage. To a greater extent than either before or since, poets and painters, novelists, essayists, and architects took the lead in promoting the importance of liberal education in forming a discerning intelligence. To some extent new men, they consistently emphasized the advantages of liberal education in achieving social and professional independence; and provided with a new theory of literary criticism, which gave them both a role and an ideology, they magnified the function of art in its relation to life. Since literature and belles lettres, painting and criticism were those areas of thought in which some of the most sensitive explorations of the meaning of art for life were occurring, the aesthetic emphasis in a liberal education was reinforced. Once again, the meaning of a liberal education was intricately connected to the most vital cultural changes of the period.

[1] George Pellew, *The Life and Correspondence of the Rt. Honorable Henry Addington, First Viscount Sidmouth*, III (London, 1847), 487.

7

Sociability

═══

EVERY AGE has its model of an educated man, be he warrior, cleric, philosopher, or research scientist. From the Italian Renaissance, 'down to a time which is within the memory of men still living', the ideal that was most publicized in Europe was the cortegiano, the courtier or the statesman. The ideal survived the destruction of republican Italy, went on to perform service in the courts of princely Italy, and was imported into England and offered to the monarchs of the Reformation period. The religious, constitutional, and political difficulties of the sixteenth and seventeenth centuries, however, did not allow it to prosper, but by the eighteenth century it was still very much alive and ready for a final flowering.

Before the ideal could realize its potential for England, it had to clear a new obstacle. The average 'courtier' of the eighteenth century had little or no association with the court, certainly not on a daily basis. In fact, he was not a courtier at all. He was more than likely a country gentleman, a city merchant or financier, or a London professional man. The new cortegiano, as one of the historians of the courtesy tradition has noted, was therefore far less political and far more social, concerned less with the roles of courtier, philosopher-king, or statesman, and far more with the qualities of appearance and good taste.[1] The reasons for this are not hard to discover. In the scramble for political power that followed the departure of James II and saw, eventually, the arrival of a German king, many country gentlemen were pushed aside, and their political influence, locally as well as in Parliament, was reduced or neutralized. The smaller

[1] George C. Brauer, Jr., *The Education of a Gentleman; Theories of Gentlemanly Education in England, 1660–1775* (New York, 1959), 118.

59

gentry were even more vulnerable. They were squeezed eco-
nomically throughout the eighteenth century as the great landed
peers and rich influential gentry extended their holdings and
widened the gap financially and socially. What was left for the
lesser country gentlemen were the management of their estates
and the cultivation of the kind of social graces needed to divert
and enhance an enforced leisure and soften resentment. Assistance was required to accomplish this. Advice was needed on how
to conduct one's daily affairs with the least friction, how to
improve a reputation or even acquire a respectable name, and
how to get on in fashionable society, whether in London or in
style-conscious regional capitals. An *arbiter elegantiarum,* as
Dr. Johnson put it, was needed, and it was found in the genre
of the courtesy book.

In the history of liberal education the courtesy book plays an
important part. In the era of the tutor it was perhaps the most
influential, at least the most accessible, of all the kinds of books
written on education. It carried the tradition of Italian humanism,
or parts of it, through the Tudor and Stuart periods, when the
grammar schools and universities were indifferent to Renaissance
ideas of education, and it planted the cortegiano ideal in the more
hospitable Augustan soil.

The courtesy book lasted in England until 1780, after which it
disappeared, or rather, changed into the etiquette book, less
universal in tone and more specifically designed for a small
coterie of 'best people'.[1] The courtesy book was more impersonal
and less class-conscious than its nineteenth-century descendent.
Its object was typical behaviour. The genre covered many
subjects: how to write letters of advice to a son at the university,
what to read for a basic education, the place of a wife in domestic
economy, the importance of travel, and so on. Because the genre
had a long pedigree, the advice was frequently repetitive. Much
in the courtesy book was ossified, irrelevant convention, stock
sayings, platitudes, and maxims. But enough of its content was
also pertinent. Despite the clichés and conventional wisdom to
be found in its pages, change of some sort was inevitable, for

[1] John E. Mason, *Gentlefolk in the Making; Studies in the History of
English Courtesy Literature and Related Topics from 1531–1774* (Phila-
delphia, 1935), 292. But for the survival of the genre with respect to
women's education, *infra* Chapter 8.

without adjustments in the advice offered, the tradition would have ended sooner than it actually did. For the essence of the courtesy book was utility. It was basically a practical treatise or manual, a reasonably sensitive, if imperfect, indicator of changing styles, moods, fashions, and values. One of the major changes to be found in the book was in its language and overall tone. The language of the courtesy book, says Mason, who has written the most useful work on the subject, became plainer, more direct, more worldly, and more useful for the business of everyday life. The simplification of language was actually the continuation of a trend noticeable in the seventeenth century when the so-called 'plain-style' became the language of the sermon, and when, towards the end of the period, the complex metaphysical conceit ceased to be the main requirement of poetic invention.

The transformed courtesy book of the eighteenth century placed even more emphasis on manners than did its predecessors, thus reinforcing social trends already in operation. Its influence strengthened the association between education and conduct, between learning and practical affairs. From its location on the shelves of gentlemen it found its way into letters and conversation, and through the authority it possessed as the representative of an enlightened tradition of education it helped propel the age towards the paradisiacal goal of civility and liberality.

We have discussed 'civility'. 'Liberality' too has eighteenth-century meanings unfamiliar in preceding eras. In Jacobean or Caroline usage the word 'liberality' contained definite restraining connotations. Writers using it were still highly influenced by Aristotelian ethics. In the scholastic catalogue of virtues, 'liberality' described moderate or 'mean' behaviour, being an expression of generosity midway between extravagance and miserliness. The liberal man was generous but not overly so, and he was careful in expenditure but not niggardly. In all matters of giving or borrowing, the liberal man regulated his conduct by close attention to his means. He did not spend more on himself or others than he could afford; nor did he spend less.[1] This was the scholastic meaning of liberality taught in the arts curricula of the universities.

Another meaning began to penetrate outside the universities

[1] Costello, 67.

through the medium of the courtesy book. 'Liberality' as communicated this way was rather broader in meaning and purpose, referring not so much to a specific act of spending or lending but to status-related values. Liberality meant good temper in dealing with others, for this was a mark of breeding and gentlemanliness. It also meant lavish generosity, for in an age of conspicuous expenditure anything less than a policy of the open purse would have left a gentleman vulnerable to the charge of stinginess. Generosity and good temper were the attributes of a man of the world.

Related to liberality was sociability, the ability to make or keep friends, to find companions and congenial company, and to avoid at all costs either being alone, or—what in this context amounts to the same thing—offending others. 'Sociability' is actually an early nineteenth-century word. The word used widely by the Georgians was 'sociable', and to a lesser extent 'sociableness'. Bailey, in his early eighteenth-century dictionary, defines both of them as 'delighting in, or fit for Company or Conversation'. Johnson agreed that this was a good definition for 'sociableness', although he did not make it the primary meaning of 'sociable'.

'Sociableness' or sociability was as important to the Georgian idea of a liberal education as civility, and the connection between the words is obvious. Without one there could not be the other. Sociability was an anchor in uncertain London waters and an occupational necessity. Being sociable produced friends, and friends were useful in opening up career opportunities. The two uses of sociability were openly admitted. A liberal education, noted the headmaster of Dumfries School in Scotland, especially if received in a public school (by which was meant a place away from home), was useful for gaining friends and promoting friendship. And 'Friendship, by the tender sympathies which it produces, is known to heighten our joys, and to soften our cares.' But—and this is certainly as important—friendship, by 'the attachments which it forms . . . is often the means of advancing a man's fortune in the world.'[1] It was necessary to have allies or points of reference in an antic, scrambling world.

The values and ideals of social behaviour in the eighteenth

[1] George Chapman, *A Treatise on Education*, 4th ed. (London, 1790), 40.

century and the implications of these for a liberal education are
nowhere more in evidence than in the extraordinary importance
assigned to speech in general and conversation in particular. So
much of social life is organized for the purpose of enabling
conversation to take place that it is easy to overlook the forms this
took and the importance it assumed in the Georgian period. The
coffee or chocolate house, the salon, and the club were created to
group together men (and men and women) for purposes of talk.
This was to a certain extent possible because of the leisured and
luxurious existence of families of property and position, but it
was not limited to that. The economic demands of urban,
industrial living had not yet made their full impact on social
existence, and the pace of life enabled many persons, whether
very wealthy or merely comfortable, to find ample time for talk.
Of course, the prevalence of servants was a factor—if someone
else does the work, there is more time for chat.

The greatest biography of the period is a record, although not
just that, of conversations. The principal novels of the eighteenth
century are novels of talk, whether in the epistolary mode, or as
in the novels of Jane Austen, which perhaps close the Georgian
period, brilliant conversation pieces, wherein the various forms
of speech—dialogue, interior monologue, free indirect speech—
are used and experimented with.[1] A spur to the importance of
public speaking was provided with the renewal of vigorous
Parliamentary debate in the final quarter of the eighteenth
century. A series of international and colonial crises reawakened
representative government after the comparative silence of half a
century when debate was nominal, or at best restricted to the
legislature. Earlier, the essential business of government took
place in the court or royal closet (once in a while in a tavern), or
in the private negotiations of a few powerful men.

Never before in English society had so many persons placed a
premium on conversation as in the second half of the eighteenth
century. Even the manufacture of furniture and household
accessories attests to this. To encourage intimacy: small tables
for cards or tea. To encourage talk at length: the comfortable
broad seats and curved splats that mark the change from stiff
William III high-backed chairs to supple Queen Anne. Hot

---

[1] For an absorbing discussion see Norman Page, *The Language of Jane
Austen* (Oxford, 1972).

drinks that could not be consumed in a hurry—tea, coffee, chocolate; restful estate gardens laid out in the famous S-shaped 'line of beauty' of which Hogarth wrote, beckoning to distant surprises and inviting a leisurely walk in the shrubbery—all of these were in different ways means of promoting the same ends.

If it is true that a new social importance was attached to conversation and that the remarkable domestication of eighteenth-century landed, professional, and business families contributed fundamentally to this cultural change, it is also true that never before had so many persons valued speaking correctly and choosing words carefully. In the last decades of the eighteenth century spoken and written English were undergoing significant changes. Linguists have studied the changes and have offered suggestive conclusions. In the first part of the eighteenth century there still existed a certain grammatical freedom. Pronunciation varied. Regional dialects were spoken at all levels of society without embarrassment. A trend toward what was to be called proper or correct speech began, however, and continued throughout the eighteenth century, accelerating towards the end. Some words and phrases in common use before 1750 deteriorated in meaning, became vulgarities, and were relegated to particular portions of the population—e.g., 'sick' and 'stink'.[1] Sometimes this was done according to status or occupation, sometimes according to region, and, in the early nineteenth century, sometimes according to 'class', a word that began to acquire its present sociological meaning about that time. London speech and pronunciation assumed an importance they did not have in earlier periods, and regional dialects correspondingly lost prestige. When everyone speaks in dialect, it is not conspicuous. But when the language of the capital becomes the correct way to speak, regional patois is more noticeable, a matter either for pride or apology.

[1] Joan Platt, 'The Development of English Colloquial Idiom during the 18th Century', in *The Review of English Studies*, II (January, 1926), 70–81; (April, 1926), 189. She speculates that the cause of the deterioration in meaning of 'sick' and 'stink' was 'due to the spread of the various civilised amenities, such as personal cleanliness and privacy; the natural life was not so much to the fore and therefore came to be regarded as a matter for shame.'

The net result of the linguistic changes of the eighteenth century was the creation of what today is called Standard English. Spoken and written language were used to draw fine social distinctions between groups or individuals. Language came to reflect the moving line of social discrimination, and the use of words became a means of moving that line. Finally, the emphasis on individual speech no longer made it so apparent which group or class someone belonged to.

While these developments were occurring, the study of rhetoric also changed. Rhetoric, historically the companion of logic, both together comprising the study of how ideas are exchanged, became in certain elegant circles delivery or pronunciation, the cultivation of a pleasant or graceful style. Quintilian and Cicero were expressly read for this purpose. Thomas Sheridan, the elocutionist father of the playwright, told his audiences that correct pronunciation 'is a sort of proof that a person had kept good company, and on that account is sought after by all, who wish to be considered as fashionable people, or members of the beau monde.'[1] In the universities of Oxford and Cambridge the change meant that declamations, required of undergraduates from time to time as part of their education in the colleges, became more concerned with manner than with matter.

Non-English authors played an interesting role in the movement to promote a standard English. Many of the principal publicists were Scottish and Irish, men like George Campbell or Hugh Blair and the members of the Scottish common sense school in general, or the Dublin elocutionist, Thomas Sheridan, from whom we have just heard. The reasons for their participation are not difficult to discern. London, which had long been a political and administrative capital, had only recently become a cultural and imperial capital. A national or imperial culture requires a common language and standard of expression. Ambitious young men, drawn to London from provincial areas, were anxious to acquire the latest style of speech and dress and to drop regional mannerisms and identifications which they considered backward and inferior. Standard English flourished as regional culture declined. The process was interrelated.

The creation of a Standard English in a kingdom where there

[1] Wilbur Samuel Howell, *Eighteenth-Century British Logic and Rhetoric* (Princeton, 1971), 240.

were great regional differences in syntax, idiom, and pronunciation had an influence on the spread of literacy generally. Undoubtedly, the growth of periodicals, radiating outwards from what by the end of the century would be called 'literary London' or 'literary Edinburgh', hastened the changes. Language change was promoted by litterateurs and journalists, whether in London or in the rapidly growing centres of a provincial press; and it was also promoted by scholars and schoolmasters, by grammarians, rhetoricians and logicians, lexicographers and elocutionists—all of whom were loud and active in the final decades of the eighteenth century.

In view of these special and, it can be said, unprecedented changes, it is not surprising that the teaching of language should have assumed a central place in the curriculum that comprised a liberal education. It might, however, be expected that the teaching of English would have taken precedent over the teaching of classical languages, especially as an increasing geographical mobility made it apparent how much variation in pronunciation occurred in English as spoken in Scotland, Ireland, and America. Indeed, the teaching of English was regarded as important to a liberal education, especially in the Dissenting academies, but this did not push the teaching of classical languages out of the limelight. In fact, the developing interest in a 'correct' English provided yet another justification for the teaching of Latin grammar and syntax. Scholars regarded Latin as a perfect language and precisely the model required to purge English of its many impurities. It was not until Sir William Jones demonstrated much later in the century that all languages developed historically, that a quintessential language was impossible, that the schoolmaster's confidence in Latin's linguistic perfection was challenged. But even when that happened, there was always the connection between classical languages and Taste to fall back on.

To our ears much of Georgian talk was small. To place the conversational ideal in proper historical perspective, however, it is necessary for us to recall the function of speech in the eighteenth century. Conversation was tied to sociability, the foremost purpose of a liberal education. As such, it was given an axiological as well as a functional purpose. It was also the key to understanding character, and thus one determinant of moral worth.

Action alone was not a sufficient criterion for measuring virtue in late Georgian England. In the country, where the principal diversions were riding, hunting, dining, churchgoing, the household arts, cards, neighbourly calls and occasional parties, balls, or theatricals, action was stereotyped or conventional. The true test of personal worth was conversation, the means by which the interrelationships of persons were furthered. But not only in the country was conversation important. In London, a city of strangers, where all relationships were uncertain to begin with, the new conventions of speech gave some assurance of stability and common values.

We can gain some further insight into the purpose of a liberal education if we ask ourselves what the Georgians thought would be the consequences of being without it. What, in fact, were the characteristics of the man lapsed into savagery or the low born person who had never succeeded in overthrowing the marks of his subordination?

There were first of all political consequences. It was an honored platitude and a worthy belief of the eighteenth-century Englishman that he was a free man in a free country, and he made a direct connection between a liberal education and the love of liberty by associating the illiberal man with tyranny. A sometime Cambridge fellow wrote in 1759: 'A man bred a slave is educated to become a tyrant, when power devolves to him. The transition is necessary and sudden, and admits of no intermediate state of natural popular freedom.'[1]

Richard Davies is talking specifically about the low status sizars and servitors at Cambridge and Oxford, the menials of the colleges, and warning that smouldering resentment at their treatment by the rich would in the course of time show itself when they became fellows. There is a touch of Nietzsche's slave morality in this description: he who was once a slave will try to enslave others. A liberal education engendered a love of liberty: through this door entered the Commonwealth or Country tradition of political ideology that crisscrossed the Atlantic in the course of the eighteenth century.

The servile man who had not been emancipated through a liberal education, who had not been rendered sociable, was a

---

[1] Quoted in Knox, *Liberal Education*, 128.

slave psychologically; in a phrase of more recent coinage, he wore his chains inside. This had an obvious effect on his behaviour, which, however expressed, amounted to the same thing—that he was unfit for human society and unfit even to live with himself. The warped or twisted personality makes his appearance everywhere in eighteenth-century literature; and to underscore the point, the Georgians carried over into their own plays the dramatic idea of a 'reigning' or 'ruling' passion which had its roots in seventeenth-century physiological theory.

The servile man was not generous. On the contrary, he was, as Johnson said, 'mean' or parsimonious, clinging to his coins, lending reluctantly. He was consistently petty-minded and narrow in his behaviour, quick to find fault, quarrelsome, captious, nitpicking, morose. Instead of avoiding offence, he sought it. The tyranny he attempted to impose on others was proof of his inferior origins and ill-breeding, and all were manifestations of illiberality.

The characteristics of the illiberal, ungenerous, unsociable man are easy enough to extend. A kind of cultural elision is in some respects a key to the list. Ill breeding easily becomes identified with inferior birth, penny-pinching is associated with tyranny, a want of affability is a sign of servility, and so on. But there is a necessary deduction. If the purpose of a liberal education was to enable a man to get along in the company of others— in fact, to make companionship itself possible and to make life pleasant when there was so much abroad to make it sour—then the absence of a liberal education produced a dangerous state of social alienation, withdrawal, and isolation, destructive to self and society. The fear of such a person is deeply rooted in Georgian culture and gives a dark, even ominous, lining to the theory of behaviour so strongly associated with politeness. It produced a disbelief in the value of privacy and a correspondingly heavy emphasis on conduct in public. The moralist and essayist Bernard Mandeville noted this tendency with some approval, for social conformity was a desirable end. But a few years later the theologian, William Law, in describing several of the consequences of 'our modern education', concluded that social convention was a disruptive rather than an integrative influence, and Rousseau, although he partly changed his mind, carried the idea in a new direction by criticizing civilized man, *l'homme sociable*, for existing on the opinions of others. At the same time he praised primitive man for being able to live privately, for drawing nourishment from his own inner resources.[1]

There are several ways in which the fear of privacy, the dislike of isolation, and suspicion of withdrawal can be intimated. Literary and poetic discussions of gardens and other sylvan or pastoral retreats are useful for this purpose, especially because the garden in western civilization is more than symbol or metaphor: it also carries theological and ethical meaning.

In the second quarter of the seventeenth century the garden became a favourite image of poets and writers who associated it with the joyous life to which a happy man could retire, turning his back on the political difficulties of court and crown. The dominant conception of the garden in the reigns of the early Stuarts was an Elysian Field, and even more, a Garden of Eden, where ordered, harmonious nature, luxuriant in careful cultivation, enclosed the happy man and protected him from the rank weeds of field and politics.[2]

The notion of retirement became in time a cult and persisted well into the eighteenth century: the poet in his grotto at Twickenham, the philosopher in his study, the gentleman on his estate, the Londoner in relief making for the country—all fleeing the world when it was too much for them. In the move from Jacobean to Georgian England, however, an important shift occurred in the image of the garden. The heavenly garden became a terrestrial one even more determinedly pagan than the Elysian Fields, Eden gave way to Athens, and the meaning of withdrawal took on an important ambivalence. The garden of Bacon, Marvell, Milton, Mildmay Fane, Nathaniel Whiting, Nicholas Hookes and countless other writers major and minor, a paradise for happy men, became the anxious retreat of Cowley, Evelyn, and Temple; not the residence of Adam and Eve before the Fall, but the garden where the hedonist and atheist Epicurus hid himself from prying eyes.

The philosophy of Epicurus was revived in the reign of Charles II, and the views attributed to the Hellenic philosopher received a mixed reception in the Restoration. For scientists Epicurean

[1] Arthur O. Lovejoy, *Reflections on Human Nature* (Baltimore, 1961), 231–42.
[2] Hill, 349–50, 350n.

writings were one source of the atomistic physical theories originating in ancient Greece, although Epicurus himself got them from Democritus and Leucippus. For moralists the word 'epicurean' seemed to sum up the dissipation of the restored Stuart court. For psychologists epicurean thought was important in the formation of the materialistic presuppositions of Lockean epistemology. But for the social and cultural history of privacy Epicurus and his garden have rather a different importance. Although the garden had some of the ambivalent attractions of its Hebraic counterpart, being both a place of danger and a place of bliss, in general it was believed to be a seductive, sinful influence. Epicurus did not have a good press in antiquity or in the Christian era. It was suspected in his own time and afterwards that the house and grounds in Athens were scenes of secret pleasures, and when after many centuries Sir Epicure Mammon stepped upon the Jacobean stage, the suspicion was renewed.

The reasons for retiring from the world took many forms in the century from Cromwell to George III. There were squires who sat out the civil wars, courtiers out of favour at the Restoration, the party out of power in the reign of Queen Anne, the politician out of favour in the ensuing 'Robinocracy' of Walpole, the writer who lost his patronage, the litterateur disgusted with the corruption, disease, and gossip of snarled London. Whatever reason might underlie the desire for privacy and isolation, the man of affairs always had to contend with the bad reputation of Epicurus' garden. Those who watched him withdraw explained his retirement as defeat, humiliation, or even the avoidance of the high responsibilities of public life. Perhaps he was also indulging a private lust.

The decision to retire, therefore, was not one that a gentleman made easily. Before he elected the life of contemplation, he had to weigh the opprobrium that would inevitably pursue his decision, and we can speculate on the amount of strain and anxiety the problem of withdrawal produced. But once having made the decision, the gentleman retiring to the country (or, as we shall see, to Oxford and Cambridge) could draw upon another and happier recollection of Epicurus' garden. It was not at all a place of clandestine evil. It was a sanctuary from the world's wickedness, where dignity could be maintained in the face of disappointment, or where calm and philosophic detachment could be regained far from the madding crowd (the phrase was Georgian before Hardy used it). In the country or in his garden, watching the apricots or figs ripen on the wall, he could await the call, as in the early nineteenth century Grey waited for it on the eve of the Reform Bill, secure in his georgic virtue.

The dislike of privacy can be illuminated in another way, one that bears more directly on the organization of education. More and more in the eighteenth century the school, as opposed to instruction at home, was advocated as the proper locus of education. Although the century began with Locke's influential recommendation of tutorial instruction, his arguments were less persuasive as the values of civility and sociability spread, assuming so many shapes and patterns. The disadvantages of home education were contrasted with the benefits of school, or what was called 'public' education. At home the child was removed from society. He was deprived of the kind of education needed to shine in company. In order to acquire a genuine liberal education, said the schoolmasters, the child had to be removed to a more sociable, emancipating setting. (Of course, they did not add that they were as interested in shillings as in children.)

In criticizing instruction received in the home, schoolmasters were criticizing tutors, and they did so with the conscious intention of exploiting the ambiguous status of hired teachers. Tutors, although often persons of clerical standing, were nevertheless likely to be treated like servants. And servants, as everyone knew, were low-born, ill-mannered, superstitious—in a word, servile.

Association with the servant class would have presented no particular difficulties in earlier centuries when service, either domestic or in husbandry, virtually enjoined membership in the employing family, and when young servants were commonly treated as if they were the masters' own children. But in the eighteenth century, and especially in London, what can be called the traditional master-servant relationship underwent striking change. London domestics of all ranks began to feel the effects of a dynamic, commercial society, in which they were in short supply relative to demand. They perceived opportunities for social mobility simply unknown in distant rural parishes. The result was a rupture in the values governing service relationships. Conflicts, which customarily had been subsumed under traditional patterns of familial authority, now broke into the open. London footmen even went so far as to form a proto-employees organization in the second half of the eighteenth century. But while servants in general perhaps gained in self-esteem by acquiring a greater independence, they lost in reputation and status. The word 'servant' itself shows this. It underwent linguistic degradation and deterioration in the late eighteenth century. Having once been used to describe the personal attendants of the privileged classes, the word came to mean a domestic person generally, with the clear implication that domestics served families of inferior social standing.[1]

Because servants were no longer members of the family, because their employment, being contractual, was somewhat indefinite, and because their loyalty could no longer be counted upon, schoolmasters could argue that the home was not a suitable place for the inculcation of values like civility and liberality. Children, in daily contact with servants, perhaps even taught by them, were in constant danger of acquiring bad habits and manners. And in making their case, schoolmasters were, of course, drawing on assumptions about the purposes and methods of liberal education that were virtually inseparable from a myriad of other cultural values deeply buried in the whole of Georgian society.

It is conventional to mock Georgian sociability as a comedown from the higher ideals of preceding ages, when morality was still rooted in religion, or when service to the State was an animating component of political theory. Moral considerations, however, were never absent from the minds of writers or artists in Georgian England. In fact, moral didacticism is one of the most obvious characteristics of the century. But it is true that in certain respects there was a fall. Among the élite groups moral improvement became associated with agreeable behaviour. In many intellectual and in the leading fashionable circles virtue was linked to Tully instead of to God, as classical learning and Christian theology parted company in the eighteenth century. It is easy to understand why after the sectarian conflict of the later seventeenth century and the theological quarrels that

[1] Platt, 81; Peter Laslett, *The World We Have Lost* (London, 1965), 2, 3, 12, 13, 20, 69; J. Jean Hecht, *The Domestic Servant Class in Eighteenth-Century England* (London, 1956), 77–87.

spilled over into the early eighteenth century, the morality of
Hobbes and the scepticism of Hume, Georgians preferred a more
congenial or hedonistic set of social ideals.

Georgian sociability has also been attacked because it was
superficial, snobbish, and depreciated learning. It is true that this
was apparently the case. Appearances were everything, or nearly
everything. But to be fair to the Georgians, we must recall the
ideal of civilization towards which they were continually striving,
trying always with unavoidable strain to approximate in daily
relations universal standards of conduct.

In the eighteenth century the purpose of a liberal education
was to produce a social type whose independence was expressed
as generosity, amiability, and liberality. Sociability—the Golden
Rule (the motto of all utilitarians, palaeo as well as neo)—also
implied 'the minuter duties and inferior decencies', and the signs
of good breeding and a proper education were easily discerned in
manners. A premium was placed on putting others at ease,
either for the pleasure it gave both, or for some advantage that
could be expected to follow. Friends were needed, so the arts of
being in company had to be cultivated. Besides, the stress of
getting on, as Professor Lowenthal comments, made relaxation
quite as important as moral uplift.[1] To entertain, to be entertained, to be entertaining: these objectives were highly valued.
And they were to be attained through balls, plays, musical
evenings, salons, dinners—the pleasures of society.[2] Clergymen
in rural retreats, who may have once had some direct experience
of these pleasures, longed for them, at times, we may imagine,
to the detriment of their parishioners. While the high-born were
obviously central figures in the dissemination of a courtier-
gentleman ideal, they were by no means the only persons
regarded as suitable recipients of a polite education. 'Gentlemen
be made cheap' in Hanoverian as in Tudor England; and the

[1] Lowenthal, 105.

[2] The moral weight of agreeable diversion is well indicated by the following illustration from a Scot pleased by the establishment of a Poker Club
in Edinburgh in 1762. Founded for 'national purposes'—i.e., to bring
together representatives of the leading social groups or strata, club
meetings 'had also Happy Effects on Private Character by Forming and
polishing the Manners which are Suitable to Civilis'd Society.' Alexander
Carlyle, *Anecdotes and Characters of the Times* (London, 1973), 282.

73

polite circles of the eighteenth century were many and varied. Liberality of behaviour was socially functional in several critical ways: to ameliorate the anomie and violence of exploding London and to avoid giving rise to the suspicion that one was low born or servile. The suspicion was easy to arouse: the age was both a time of expanding opportunities for social mobility and the heyday of the rogue or con man (or woman), well publicized in contemporary literature.

8

Oxford, Cambridge and a Liberal Education in the Eighteenth Century

———

In the eighteenth century a liberal education did not assume, and certainly did not require, residence at a university. One of the outstanding features of liberal education in the Georgian period is the many institutional forms that it could take. A liberal education could be offered in boarding or grammar schools, or in Dissenting academies and private educational establishments, or it could be acquired by the wealthy on a grand tour of the continent. Locke thought a tutor would provide it, and while his influence lasted tutorial instruction was one major source of liberal instruction. But the advance of the ideal of sociability through the second half of the eighteenth century challenged his advice, as parents worried more and more about the isolation of their sons from the great world. Autodidacticism was ruled out on similar grounds.

The absence of any *de facto* university direction over the organization of secondary education allowed a considerable amount of educational independence in the determination of programmes of study. Entirely literary in character, focused particularly on the study of classical languages, and requiring therefore only a few cardinal texts, a liberal education did not depend on major research libraries or extensive collections of books. It did not require dons or professors or degrees. Any teacher, provided he had some Latin, a little learning, and the right manner, could undertake the task of liberal instruction. Each headmaster was free to promote (and if he chose, publish) his views on liberal education in an effort to attract pupils without worrying about any of the university constraints that were to appear in the nineteenth century. Most students did not have to

75

go from school to university in order to complete their education. Admission to the university, for those who did attend (and they were relatively few), did not depend upon meeting a range of preliminary requirements, and the universities did not object to remedial instruction once undergraduates were in residence. Remedial instruction was welcomed, in fact, for it meant additional employment for idle fellows, and it was handsomely remunerated. There were scholarship students in the eighteenth century, but the entrance standard for them was really no higher than for ordinary students. Only a few Oxbridge colleges had anything resembling a scholarship examination, and no one complained of its severity. Most of the scholarship payments were restricted to particular schools or regions, and the least important of the criteria for admission was proficiency or promise.

The experimentation was greatest in non-Anglican schools, since the Dissenting community, effectively barred from Church of England institutions, was totally free to establish its own standards; but even traditional grammar schools showed initiative. Modern languages like Italian were taught at one period in Hull's history, and the schools in Leicestershire also showed a certain amount of enterprise. Hawkshead in the Lake District developed excellent teaching in mathematics. While this is perhaps an example of where the influence of a university was important—Hawkshead was one of the Cambridge feeder schools, and the teaching of mathematics was centred in Cambridge—the number of schools thus influenced was not great. Supplementary private instruction in mathematics for Cambridge undergraduates early became the rule. In most older schools Latin and sometimes Greek formed the teaching spine, but other subjects were known and promoted. The courtesy books of the eighteenth century, always sensitive to possible changes in educational taste, often had a place for non-classical subjects, for natural or experimental science, modern history, and modern languages. The legitimacy of these subjects is uncertain. While some writers included them in the category of liberal subjects, others thought them unnecessary for sons destined for the Church or public life. Apparently the teaching of modern subjects was prevalent enough to bring this complaint from the author of an important late eighteenth-century treatise on liberal

education: 'Ariosto, Tasso, and Boileau, are to be read in preference to Homer, Virgil, and Horace; and the works of Voltaire
alone to be substituted in the place of all the poetry, all the
philosophy, and all the history that has ever been written. In
consequence of these mistaken notions, our great grammar-
schools, which have produced so many ornaments of human
nature, are exploded, by the frivolous and insolent, as the seats
of illiberal manners, of antiquated learning, and, in a word, of
pedantry.'[1]

Perhaps the main historical reasons for the failure of the
universities to take the lead in promoting liberal education were
political. The action taken by the Tudors to safeguard the
Reformation in England entangled Church and State, and since
the universities were already in some respects ecclesiastical
institutions, the Erastian arrangements of the sixteenth century
meant that a political presence in the universities was unavoidable. The result was a university often called upon to protect the
presumed interests of Church and State and kept from innovation, even right into Georgian times, by the interference of royal
courts. When control of the English State passed to the landed
aristocracy in the eighteenth century, the ensuing mixture of lay,
spiritual, and royal patronage also prevented the universities
from undertaking constructive reform. The incentive for change
was consistently absent. Other educational institutions were
freer to innovate and did so. Educational leadership passed out
of the universities into the more dynamic sections of English
society. Georgian ideals of a liberal education were developed
by a new group of publicists and belles lettrists and incorporated
into a new urban and urbane culture. Italian humanist ideas,
however modified, reinforced by the writings of seventeenth-
century French courtesy authors, at long last found a ready,
widespread reception. Oxford and Cambridge had to defend
themselves as best they could against the charge that their
education was medieval and scholastic, not Renaissance and
liberal, and that the last places in which a young man could
receive a proper liberal education were the shaded, isolated,
monkish courts of the universities.

The criticism of Oxbridge education began with the ends of

[1] Vicesimus Knox, *Essays, Moral and Literary*, I (London, 1815), 15.

liberal education and worked backwards to the means. Since the purpose of liberal education was to produce civilized persons, instructed in the workings of the laws of human nature, able to make their way through the intricacies of Georgian social behaviour and establish the right tone in all social encounters, it followed that education without sociability as its goal was unsatisfactory. An Oxbridge education was illiberal because neither the teaching nor the academic exercises nor the general atmosphere of the colleges enabled young men to be at ease in the world. No matter which texts were studied, claimed the detractors, they were not studied in such a way as to further the true ends of liberal education. In a word, the Oxbridge curriculum was not sufficiently 'useful' to meet the practical requirements of polite education.

While there were many attacks on the university curriculum, they all pointed in one way or another to the teaching of logic. In the official curricula of both Oxford and Cambridge, logic was the central subject. No student, unless he were a nobleman, could take a degree without undergoing an examination in logic, or rather, to use the correct medieval designation, without 'disputing' in the schools. The problem was not that logic and argument, the ability to think connectedly and to keep to the point, were devalued by critics outside the universities. On the contrary, logic was an essential ingredient of all humanist writings on education, an indispensable part of the intellectual training of the cortegiano or statesman. Furthermore, rhetoric, the companion to logic in the old university *trivium* and *quadrivium*, was also the most important feature of Italian humanist learning. The difficulty was not that logic and rhetoric were illiberal subjects, but that the universities made them so: first, by emphasizing scholastic forms of logical analysis when progressive eighteenth-century writers were looking to modern logicians like John Locke, or were more interested in Roman rhetoricians like Cicero and Quintilian than in Attic ones like Aristotle; and second, by equating reasoning with disputing and rhetoric with declaiming. Somehow the schoolmen were alive, if not well, in an age of enlightenment and humane learning.

The survival of peripatetic logic in the history of Oxford and Cambridge is indeed an extraordinary tale. When Italian Renaissance learning first arrived in England at the beginning of the sixteenth century, it did not seem that the scholastic curriculum would survive the competition. Under the influence of humanist representatives in England like Erasmus and Colet, it appeared certain that the traditional university course of subjects would be overthrown. But the conventional teaching subjects demonstrated surprising tenacity and survived every new challenge. Despite the later arrival of the 'new science' and the foundation of new chairs, 'undergraduates' (a neologism of the sixteenth century to describe a new category of collegiate student) were examined in the scholastic programme of studies throughout the Tudor and Jacobean periods. In the later seventeenth century, following the example of the Ramist school in France, English university scholars de-emphasized certain Aristotelian features of logic; but in the 1690s Dean Aldrich of Christ Church, Oxford, while undertaking a number of revisions, essentially restored the traditional emphasis. Consequently, the Aristotelian influence on Oxford students steadily remained throughout the eighteenth century, and flourished in the early nineteenth century, when Richard Whately built on Aldrich's foundations to give Oxford a really superior school of logic once again.

A rival system to Aldrich's, and one more congenial to Georgian critics of the universities, developed simultaneously under the leadership of Locke. His object was to correct conventional methods of proof which were largely verbal by adding a factual dimension, a procedure generally uncharacteristic of preceding logical systems. According to Wilbur Samuel Howell, the historian of eighteenth-century logic, Locke tied his system of logic to the inductive sciences and separated it from the humanities, while Aldrich, remaining within the university tradition, insisted that logic retain its conventional association with the liberal arts.[1]

It would not be correct to conclude that Locke remained entirely outside the ancient universities in the eighteenth century when he was actually widely read by students and dons, especially at Cambridge, where his logical theories were in keeping with a developing interest in the mathematical sciences. But it is certainly indicative of the loyalty that Cambridge

[1] Howell, 280.

seemed to pay peripatetic logic in its disputations to note how much care was taken even there to avoid calling the attention of undergraduates to precisely those passages in Locke where he disagreed with scholastic philosophy and berated the school-men.[1] Embarrassing passages were omitted in teaching or otherwise smoothed over.

An age that had discovered fresh sources of interest in the classics and that was pioneering new forms of fiction and historical writing was understandably impatient with what appeared to be an overly solicitous Oxbridge concern with medievalisms. The age was also dissatisfied with the whole manner in which teaching was carried on. Students, forced to prepare for the scholastic disputations, were taught to argue for the sake of argument and to 'wrangle' (a word that was also beginning to be used to indicate a certain category of Cambridge student). Unfortunately, the whole purpose of logic and rhetoric seemed misunderstood. For the civilized gentleman of the eighteenth century logic and rhetoric did not mean disputing or splitting hairs. The purpose of studying logic was not to learn to win disputes according to a particular system of reason-ing, or even to persuade; the purpose was to communicate, to bring persons together, not divide them, to teach them to be open-minded, not intolerant. Instead of learning the arts of conversation in order to be agreeable in society, students were being instructed in methods of reasoning guaranteed to lose them friends and gain enemies. A liberal education was supposed to be broadening, but Oxbridge teaching was narrow, a matter of outmoded rules. A liberal education was supposed to emphasize clarity and elegance of thought; instead, students were taught to obfuscate and start hares. A liberal education was supposed to make its recipients attentive to the needs of others; instead, students were taught to be academic snobs, to forget that a little learning was a dangerous thing, and that ultimately a great deal of learning could only be acquired outside the universities in the great world of public affairs.

The word that summed up all the distaste Georgian critics had for an Oxford or Cambridge education was 'pedantry'. This was their favourite term of abuse, a synonym for fussy scholar-

[1] Hans Aarsleff, *The Study of Language in England, 1780–1860* (Prince-ton, 1966), 118n.

ship, self-absorption, and useless learning. One well-known rhetorician of the period even drew a mordant analogy between 'the pedant in literature' and the 'hypocrite in religion.'[1] Included in the indictment of pedantry was an ongoing reaction to the virtuoso movement that had flourished in the latter part of the seventeenth century. The virtuosi had come close to realizing that most elusive of all educational ideals: learning and knowledge for their own sake. But in the estimation of another generation and another age, their zeal miscarried. The virtuoso was considered deficient in Taste and unable to discriminate. He could not distinguish between useful and useless knowledge, and he was carried away by an uncritical enthusiasm for fabulous tales and peculiar knicknacks. At one time the representatives of a healthy interest in learning and in all the works of nature, they became the symbols of befuddled scholarship and misplaced knowledge. They were laughed at for their antiquarianism and for the eagerness with which they wandered off in search of curiosities, neglecting fundamental truths much closer to hand. In their demise the virtuosi unfortunately dragged down with them their donnish successors, whose learning was similarly regarded as irrelevant.

The pedant was the universal enemy of the civilized man of the eighteenth century. Fathers sending letters of advice to sons at the universities cautioned them against the dangers of pedantry. Undergraduates were reminded of the harm it would cause their character. They were told not to lose themselves in study and to avoid specialism. As if to guard against possible pernicious influences, fathers sent along their own suggestions for reading, or corresponded with college tutors in an effort to assure that only approved books be allowed. Letters sent from fathers to sons present us with agreeable surprises. We expect the platitudes: sons are urged to study diligently, to pay attention to their tutors, choose companions wisely, comport themselves decently, and in general make good use of their time—all variations on the advice Polonius gives Laertes. But we do not expect parents to tell their sons to avoid hard work and not to endanger their health or compromise their social life by excess studying. Too much reading, they said, injured health, enforced long and lonely

[1] Howell, 611.

hours, and resulted in narrow views or prejudices, which in turn inevitably led to the irreparable loss of friends.

The sharpest attack on pedantry did not come from a critic outside the universities but from the master of one of the better colleges of the period, Samuel Powell of St. John's, Cambridge, who made the dons the special object of his rebuke. His censure of the idle monks of his university outdoes Gibbon's alliterative criticism of Oxford. Powell was high-handed in his treatment of the fellows of his college, and quite rightly they resented it. His rebuke of them may well have been an attempt to deflect criticism from what were unquestionably unpopular actions, but even if this was the case, his criticism seems valid. The generally unstimulating environment, the lack of career incentives and consequent falling off in personal ambition, and the loneliness of the bachelor community all combined, Powell wrote, to produce a cramped, bigoted, carping, paranoid, and ungenerous—that is to say, illiberal—person.[1] Here was proof from sources close to the throne that critics of Oxbridge and supporters of the principles of liberal education were correct in their assessment of the effects of a particular environment and learning on character. Fellows who escaped Oxbridge for more stimulating worlds outside echoed his sentiments. 'Taken from milk, air, and exercise, to tea, beef, and a sedentary life in College,' observed a former resident of Queen's College, Oxford, 'most of those who reside much become nervous and low-spirited. Assistance is sometimes sought from the bottle, and the bottle, like the Dane, enslaves every Britain who courts its aid and alliance. . . . Had they been hard-worked in a school [i.e., if they taught], they would have done good, probably to others, and certainly to themselves; and if they had not found a pleasure in their employment, they would have gained a superior relish for others.'[2] The characterization (or character defamation) of the don as narrow-minded and unsociable became one of the lasting stereotypes in university circles. It did not disappear until well into the nineteenth century, as the following quotation from a letter written in 1821 indicates: the dons are 'obscure pedants . . . excellent judges of an obscure passage in a Greek author—

---

[1] Thomas Smart Hughes, *Discourses by William Samuel Powell and James Fawcett* (London, 1832), 5–6, 12–13.
[2] Evans, 265.

understanding, perhaps, the value of a bottle of old port—connoisseurs in tobacco, and not wholly ignorant of the mystery of punch-making; but certainly a sort of persons [*sic*.] whom I, for one, would never wish to sit with, as assessors of the fine arts.'[1]

The Master of St. John's shared a particular fear with the parents of undergraduates. The fear was often present, although not usually named, like Cyrano's old enemy, and we can recognize its sources. It was the fear of melancholy, the great Jacobean and Georgian 'humorous' disease.

Melancholy has a fascinating social and cultural history. It was also called Nervous Distemper, the Vapours, 'hystericks', or most grandly, the Spleen, a favourite topic of eighteenth-century poets and physicians. In the seventeenth century medical writers were inclined to attribute the origins of melancholy to physical causes, principally climate. English fogs and damp and the lack of sun at least provided an explanation that was compatible with the traditional physiology of the theory of humours where heat and cold corrupted body fluids or influenced their distribution. At the beginning of the eighteenth century the theory of climate as a cause of low spirits was still widely used, but at the same time a remedy was devised which in fact profoundly contradicted the usual reasons for the source of the complaint. Increasingly melancholy was attributed to social and psychological causes.

Such an explanation was naturally in keeping with the exaggerated Georgian emphasis on the importance of everyday life in this world, with the distrust of individualism, and the dislike of any actions that could be construed as anti-social. Melancholy was regarded as an especially pernicious condition because it could lead to, and finally was considered indistinguishable from, the most important of all anti-social manifestations, madness or insanity, which rendered the individual inaccessible to reason, taste, and good sense.

Once again we cannot fail to notice the compelling cultural values which forced the Georgians to turn received traditions of thought to their own special purposes or, under the pressure of historical circumstances, to transform inherited theories. An earlier view of madness, according to a stimulating recent

[1] Pellew, 482.

account, was based on the theory of the three souls, the rational, the sensitive or passionate, and the vegetative. Insanity resulted from a personal failure to control the passions and was therefore judged to be a moral failing for which the offending individual was completely responsible. In the writings of Hobbes, Descartes, and Locke, this explanation was largely discarded. For them the problem of insanity was more than a question of the power of reason to restrain the excesses of the imagination within the individual mind. It was also a question of the influence of the environment or the world external to mind. Hobbes, of course, was troubled by the problem of the maintenance of political authority, and for him insanity bore a relationship to anarchy. Locke, who also worried about the stability of society, hoped that he could find some environmental explanation for the juxtaposition of wrong ideas that produced the madman's view of the universe.[1]

In the writings of the great Augustan thinkers madness and all its related forms, orders, ranks, and degrees became a social problem. Discussed widely, it was also picked up by the new popular press with its eye for sensation, and soon the conclusion was broadcast that the English were essentially a melancholic people with suicidal tendencies. Foreign observers like Voltaire repeated the conclusion, and by the middle of the eighteenth century the 'English malady' was a commonplace of European opinion.[2]

There is not a shred of statistical evidence to justify the conclusion that the Georgians produced an unusual number of suicides, and so it has rightly been exposed as a myth. Yet we cannot entirely dismiss the problem. Eighteenth-century England was a society undergoing dynamic transformation, requiring adjustments to new urban settings, to new mobility patterns, and to a new role in world affairs. Furthermore, the unprecedented extension of the patronage system, the pervasive role of 'influence', and the importance of connections, combined

[1] Michael V. DePorte, *Nightmares and Hobbyhorses: Swift, Sterne, and Augustan Ideas of Madness* (San Marino, California, 1974), 6–50, 50n.

[2] Oswald Doughty, 'The English Malady of the Eighteenth Century', in *The Review of English Studies*, II (July, 1926), and Roland Bartel, 'Suicide in Eighteenth-Century England: The Myth of a Reputation', *Huntington Library Quarterly*, XXIII (February, 1960).

with rising expectations, closed off opportunities for ambitious sons, producing frustration and bitterness. Adjustments in personal relationships, to include those of husbands and wives, parents and children, produced strains, anxieties, and tensions throughout English society. These are difficult, perhaps impossible to measure statistically, but their existence is undeniable. Consequently it is appropriate to look upon the concern with melancholy as more than a sensationalist circulation campaign by a free but irresponsible press. Undoubtedly journalists distorted the problem, but that it was a social and cultural problem, penetrating many levels of society, is indicated by the appearance of new remedies. Physicians advised visits to watering places in order to relax anxious patients, and Bath sprang to life again. The novelists, especially Fielding and Sterne, claimed that literature, particularly the novel, would eliminate low spirits by providing diverting entertainment.[1] Locke said that education was the answer, for the proper combination of experiences and learning would prevent insanity by eliminating its cause. Other writers said that idleness was the cause of melancholy, and Dr. Powell of St. John's agreed, advising atrabilious fellows and students to spend more time in study, but many parents worried that the true cause of spleen was loneliness. The remedy for laziness, hard work, brought with it the unfortunate side effect of pedantry. As such, it was unacceptable. The remedy for loneliness was easy enough to prescribe in an age of entertaining. All the good doctors of the university agreed that the most effective treatment that could be devised for a strange disease with unique symptoms was the pleasure and not the avoidance of company. Certainly quarantine would never do.

Melancholy began to vanish as a social disease late in the eighteenth century, first outside the universities and only much later within them. In the last decades of the century commentators noted that the English malady was without foundation, that the number of suicides in England was no greater than elsewhere. The whole problem of melancholy underwent a cultural transformation, and it was unnecessary to find a cure for what was no longer a disease but a sign of health. Some writers were connecting melancholy to a higher experience and

[1] Doughty, 263.

finding in it a measure of the sublime, a heightening of private response, an emotion to be explored, not suppressed. The connection between melancholy and the sublime may very well have been strongest among Dissenters affected by the religious revivals of the second half of the century. At least in their writings, brooding is a form of religious reflection.[1] There is no doubt that melancholy, which had so often been associated with madness, acquired an entirely new importance in the Romantic period,

> Ay, in the very temple of Delight
> Veil'd Melancholy has her sov'ran shrine
> Though seen of none save him whose strenuous tongue
> Can burst Joy's grape against his palate fine;
> His soul shall taste the sadness of her might,
> And be among her cloudy trophies hung.

And when that happened the whole question of asocial behaviour assumed a dimension unknown in Georgian culture. Parents no longer worried that their sons would become melancholic through overstudy, and dons changed their pattern of work (or leisure) without fearing an attack of black bile.

The Oxbridge curriculum and the survival of scholastic forms of education were clearly unacceptable to the proponents of liberal education as it developed outside the universities. In other ways, too, Oxford and Cambridge failed to provide the education suited to the cultural values of a society dominated by an extraordinarily influential landed aristocracy.

The theory of a liberal education, being a theory of character formation, stressed the education of the whole man. The courtesy book held up the model of a gentleman whose mind and manners were in perfect accord, whose deportment as much as his intellect or knowledge was an indication of proper education. The man intended for society had to have all dimensions of his personality suitably cultivated, and hence all aspects of his education were important, the employment of his leisure time as well as his formal studies.

The courtesy books had specified a number of recreations

[1] Pittock, 42, 43, 91, 117, 120. I have made the connection between religious reflection and melancholy rather more explicit than she does in her inestimable book. See also Houghton, 63-4.

essential to the development of the Renaissance personality. There were the group of sports and activities associated with the routine and ritual of court, intended, like the reading of liberal works, to produce a pleasing bearing. There were activities like dancing that improved the social graces and at the same time— no easy trick—prepared the cortegiano for war. When taught by a French master, said Aubrey in the late seventeenth century, dancing qualified the gentleman for conversation with ladies, prevented drunkenness, and allowed the 'commander to tread a good step and to march with a bôn grace before his company.'[1]

Fencing, dancing, riding, falconry, hunting are all mentioned at various points in the courtesy book tradition, but disagreements on their suitability for a liberal education were already present in the seventeenth century. Francis Osborn, whose book was the most widely read in his time, and continued to be read in the eighteenth century, was opposed to hunting.[2] In the eighteenth century, writers divided on the importance of dancing, some placing it in the category of music, low on the list of priorities.

Measured by the standards of the courtesy book, the recreations followed by members of the universities were not liberal. Dancing, fencing, gymnastics, and other polite or quasi-polite activities took place, but they were not in high fashion at the Oxbridge colleges, and certainly not as the century progressed. Rough country sports, to include blood sports, 'rustic illiberal sports' in Chesterfield's phrase, were the principal physical activities of dons or young men with time and money to spare, and no matter what the sport or recreation, some form of betting was sure to accompany it. Gambling, however, by universal consent, was a vice—prevalent outside the universities as well as within them, but not to be condoned.

So even at the level of leisure the universities failed to sustain an environment suited to the principles of liberal education. In yet another way, the universities were considered illiberal. There were no women, or almost no women of quality, in the university community, for there were ambitious tradesmen's daughters in the towns and less reputable companions in the streets. Undergraduates, accustomed to a sister and mother at home, or to the

[1] J. E. Stephens, ed., *Aubrey on Education* (London, 1972), 39.
[2] Mason, 69 *et seq.*

solitude of a maternal aunt, missed the company of ladies when they came to reside in the colleges. It was a cruel tradition that required dons to remain celibate at a time when marriage was essential to the continuation of an aristocratic line and when even romantic love was being accorded an important place in the affections.

Of the theories of liberal education, the eighteenth-century version was probably unique in the place accorded to women in furthering the ends of liberal instruction. So striking was this development that our discussion certainly requires more information on the underlying reasons for the change. Yet so limited is our comprehension of a crucial historical development that it is barely possible to discern what must have been profound changes in feminine conduct even before the eighteenth century opened. Literary evidence from the Jacobean period suggests a new assertiveness on the part of women of higher rank. Playwrights appear to have been irritated by the efforts made by some women to keep abreast of artistic and intellectual trends, for we find unflattering stereotypes of the lady scientist, the cultivated lady, the learned lady, the lady writer, and, to sum up the distaste, the amazon.[1]

Recent studies of literacy corroborate evidence suggested by the theatre that women were beginning to challenge accepted roles. The forwardness parodied in seventeenth-century plays was related to the appearance of better-educated women. Throughout the second half of the seventeenth century illiteracy rates (as measured by the ability to sign one's name) declined strikingly, especially in the capital. Whereas 79 per cent of London women could not sign their names in the 1670s, by the end of the century only 52 per cent were illiterate. The rate fell again in the opening decades of the eighteenth century when less than half could not sign. This meant that London women in the reign of George I were as literate as men living in other parts of the island.[2] As these figures include women from all classes, we must assume substantially higher literacy rates for women of privileged origin.

It is not, however, until the eighteenth century, especially the

[1] Jean Elizabeth Gagen, *The New Woman, Her Emergence in English Drama 1600–1730* (New York, 1954).

[2] David Cressy, 'Literacy in Pre-industrial England', *Societas*, IV (Summer, 1974), 233–5.

second half, that we are on firmer ground with respect to changes in the position of English women from the comfortable sectors of society. In London the values associated with urbanity assumed the active participation of women. To women went the responsibility for creating an environment conducive to polite behaviour. They were expected to preside over the salon with wit and charm, to bring out the talents of their male guests, and to provide an occasion for the ambitious newcomer to make the kind of contacts needed to advance his career. Karl Mannheim, following the lead of Chauncey Brewster Tinker, speaks of the place of platonic love in creating an 'erotically charged atmosphere', by which both mean that the hostess was not required to be either puritan or matriarchal.[1] She was, in fact, to be stimulating in a frankly rococo setting.

Yet it is not the erotic role but a moral one that dominates eighteenth-century discussions of the position of women either inside or outside the home. In fact the erotic, rococo model of conduct that appeared early in the eighteenth century was overturned precisely because, by stimulating passion, it was in conflict with the stronger, developing ideals of self-restraint—that is to say, the triumph over brute instinct. In the second half of the eighteenth century aristocratic hedonism was challenged by new concepts of propriety, especially in gentry families living down a reputation for hard-drinking and rude country living, or from groups rising in prestige like the clergy, or merchant and professional families moving horizontally in status. In the Georgian period, especially during the second half, women came into new prominence in the courtesy books. The misogyny which had always been part of the genre began to dissolve in response to the pressures of sociability and the importance of liberal education. In fact a whole new segment of courtesy books was created especially for women. These were still Georgian in overall character, *i.e.*, they were concerned with universal or general conceptions of conduct rather than with narrow aspects of it like etiquette. They paralleled the rise of the novel of manners, indeed, incorporated material from it. Works like *Female Conduct* by Thomas Marriott, *Sermons to Young Women* by the popular Dr. James Fordyce, or Mrs. Chapone's *Essays on the Improvement of the Mind*, as well as count-

[1] Karl Mannheim, *Essays on the Sociology of Culture* (London, 1967), 136–7.

less other letters, essays, sermons, *exempla*, and didactic fiction
became required reading for daughters uncertain of station, rank,
or deportment. An entire generation of famous women authors,
among them Jane Austen, Maria Edgeworth, Fanny Burney, and
probably the Brontës, were thoroughly acquainted with the
conduct book for women, absorbed or resisted ideas within it,
and as artists worked out for themselves the implications of such
values as self-sacrifice, chastity, modesty, or models like 'the
perfect lady' raised by their reading.[1]

Women, then, played a major part in seeing to it that the
ultimate purposes of a liberal education were achieved. Their
role was to help raise the standard of everyday behaviour and to
restrain the excesses to which men might be prone. Well-bred
men, meaning men of liberal education, were expected to requite
the attention paid to them by well-bred women. They were
expected to defer to women in public, to treat them with respect,
to talk to them (and to talk to them intelligently)—in brief, to use
the arts of civility they had supposedly learned. It is of course
possible to view the changes in interpersonal behaviour between
men and women as perhaps a different but yet another division
of sex roles. But we must at the same time recognize the cultural
magnitude of an historical movement that attempted to raise and
succeeded in raising the level of everyday personal conduct for
both men and women. If the changes that occurred then now
appear less satisfactory, as some years ago C. S. Lewis feared
they would, it may very well be a failure of historical imagination
on our part.

In Oxford and Cambridge only heads of houses married, and
the blue-stocking was not appreciated. It was only in the last
decade of the eighteenth century that individuals began to
protest the restrictions on marriage governing the award and
retention of fellowships. Opponents of celibacy argued that it
invited incontinence and sloth. Marriage, on the other hand,
promoted sexual morality and industrious behaviour. Only
monks of a barbarous and unenlightened age were celibate.
Deprived of the lawful company of women, stated one advocate
of fellowships for married dons, the monks invented salacious

---

[1] Joyce Hemlow, 'Fanny Burney and the Courtesy Books', in *Publications of the Modern Language Association*, LXV (1950), 732–61.

tales, 'ludicrous descriptions of low life and licentious manners, which we meet with in the Tales of Boccace.'[1]

These views were commonplaces of the age, and only Malthus and the Cambridge Senate came to different conclusions, although not for the same reasons. (And Malthus, as a reading of his population studies demonstrates, could not prove to his own satisfaction that celibacy guaranteed sexual continence.) But despite the protests and brief controversy, no attempt was made to alter a situation for which the historian can find only two expressed justifications: that Queen Elizabeth herself ordered celibate priests in her colleges, and that restrictions on marriage assured adequate turnover of collegiate fellowships.

Celibacy led to promiscuity, in thought as in body, to idleness, and to a coarseness of mind indicative of ill-breeding and lowly origin. This was bad enough. But there was a worse crime, for celibacy was responsible for the conditions that created potential social and political rebels. These were at least the views of an author who wrote anonymously in the period following the French regicide. A bookish environment, an indolent bachelor community without family to divert its attention, an age when too much leisure was a problem for the privileged led the collegiate fellow into—to borrow a phrase of modern sociology—'a sublimated and internalized perception of things',[2] or—to use one from the period itself—'speculations which may do no good to him, but great injury to the peace and gravity of the University.' The same writer goes on to affirm—unhesitatingly, he says—'that in general the unquiet and dissatisfied tempers, both here and in the kingdom at large, fluctuate in the breasts of unmarried men, be their departments in life ecclesiastical or civil.'[3]

As the foregoing discussion indicates, virtually every criticism of the ancient universities eventually was directed against the collegial fellowship. It was primarily in their hands that the provisions for teaching rested. It was they who were expected to carry out the educational functions provided for by pious benefactors in ages long past. The curriculum, the examinations,

---

[1] *A Letter on the Celibacy of Fellows of Colleges Addressed to the Senate* (London, 1794), 14n. Cambridge University Library, Cam.c.794.9.

[2] Mannheim, 160.

[3] *Letter on Celibacy*, 24–5.

the rough amusements, the absence of women were all no doubt indications of an illiberal environment and as such deplored, but the real problem was the dons. Pedantic, melancholic, drunken, and salacious—this was the awful portrait painted by nearly every detractor and even by representatives of the colleges. We can, of course, recognize that the accusations were not in every respect true. They were blown up for public consumption in an age of gossip and satire when overstatement was preferred, because virtue had to be sharply contrasted with vice. This was one instance of the influence of the classical moralists. But even if exaggerations, there was enough truth in the portraits to make the charges hurt. And we know that they hurt because dons were only able to muster a weak defence and because so many of the collegiate fellows chose not to reside, a practice, incidentally, for the most part contrary to statute.

The charges of illiberality made palpable hits because they exposed, or came close to exposing, the lowly or 'servile' origins of so many members of the academic community. The innuendo of low birth was directed principally at the life fellows, who were all, with minor exceptions, celibate churchmen in search of preferment. We do not as yet know a great deal about the social origins of the lesser clergy in the eighteenth century or, for that matter, the nineteenth century, but there is evidence to suggest that the jibe of inferior origin has a basis somewhere close to fact.

Undoubtedly, the overwhelming majority of dons came from clerical homes. All statistical samplings confirm an impression derived from more qualitative sources. The Church was an occupation like law or medicine in Scotland, where sons followed fathers into family occupations. One of the consequences of a married clergy in Protestant countries was the tendency for an hereditary occupation to form. This tendency was reinforced in the eighteenth century by the importance of patronage and connections. Fathers needed all possible means to find suitable employment for children, and the best place to begin was naturally with one's own positions and contacts.

In the eighteenth century there were many social strata of clergy and vast individual differences in fortune, family background, position, and style of life. But, very likely, dons tended to be recruited from the lower levels of the ecclesiastical establishment, from the parsons and stipendiary curates, rather than from the higher ranks, where, especially after 1750, the sons of landed families enjoyed a competitive advantage. The clergy from the north of England were regarded as particularly low in status and short of income, and consequently looked upon as coarse, illiberal, and ungentlemanly, at least in the estimation of the wealthy, cosmopolitan, polite south. There can be no doubt of the relative social and geographical isolation of the northern counties for most of the eighteenth century and their distance from the fashionable capital near the mouth of the Thames, and in truth the ecclesiastical revenues collected in the north were scanty. As determined by the returns of the hearth tax, the poorest counties in England in the first part of the eighteenth century were Derbyshire, Cheshire, Yorkshire, Lincolnshire, Northumberland, Durham, and Cumberland. So few were the attractions of country livings in the north that incumbents were absent. In 1743, nearly half the priests of the 836 parishes in the diocese of York were non-resident, and still another 40 per cent of the livings were held in plurality.[1]

As this was the situation in the north, small wonder that at both Oxford and Cambridge a distinct dislike was taken to the northerner who brought with him manners regarded as awkward, a dialect that was considered rude, and a personality avoided as prickly. The northerner named most often was the Yorkshireman. Lord Macaulay, in his snide remarks on regional accents in the celebrated Third Chapter, was merely repeating a prejudice that had become common in the course of the eighteenth century. Undoubtedly, failure to shed regional mannerisms was a handicap in the race for jobs outside the universities, particularly as half the benefices in England and Wales were falling into the hands of lay improprietors who demanded more than New Testament Greek as a test for preferment. Succession to college livings presented fewer obstacles to the unstylish parson, but his presence in the colleges certainly did not enhance their reputation for *civilité*.

Unquestionably, too, the don from a lower income background could not be as generous with his purse as wealthier members of the university community, and he failed to measure up to the

[1] John D. Gay, *The Geography of Religion in England* (London, 1971), 69–71.

standards of a liberal education in this way. One may note how many collegiate quarrels in the eighteenth century were over money, as represented by livings and the right of succession to livings. And as the remarks of Richard Radcliffe quoted earlier indicate, more was at stake than merely income.

Relatively low birth, then, or the suspicion of it, lack of means, regional handicaps of a cultural nature, and dependence on others for career chances all conspired against the collegiate fellows and constituted a slur on their liberality. Small wonder that they waited, often with extraordinary patience and a psychological cost that we have yet to measure, for that vacancy in a college living or for the right student from the right family in order to escape the universities and enter into a brighter world outside.

Far from the urbanity of the capital, Oxbridge dons lived in buildings which reminded critics of medieval cloisters: isolated, separate, inward-looking.[1] It was easy enough to believe that dons, like their colleges, were survivals from darker ages, and that the buildings suited the inhabitants. Or it was possible to believe that the gardens of Oxford and Cambridge were like the gardens of Epicurus, where the fellows, completely out of touch with the world at large, passed their days irresponsibly and spent their nights in accomplished debauchery. The reproach of unworldliness hung on for many decades. As late as 1833 we find a clergyman being recommended for a chair at the new University of Durham not only for his competence in mathematics, which was reasonable if not dazzling, but also because 'He has by no means the air and manners of a mere recluse; but seems to me to combine very well the character and habits of the gentleman and practical philosopher, with those of the student and the clergyman.'[2]

[1] Architecturally this was not necessarily true. The monastic architectural origin of the courts of Cambridge and quadrangles of Oxford has long been in dispute. Although Jesus College, Cambridge, may very well have been adapted from a nunnery, the models for other collegiate buildings have been traced back to the fifteenth-century manor house. See Robert Willis and John Willis Clark, *The Architectural History of the University of Cambridge, and of the Colleges of Cambridge and Eton*, 4 vols. (Cambridge, 1886).

[2] Letter from Christopher Wordsworth, Master of Trinity College, Cambridge, to the Bishop of Durham, 3 June 1833, Jenkyns Papers, Balliol College Library, Oxford.

The nadir in the status of the clerical dons was most probably in the middle decades of the eighteenth century or just when the Georgian theory of a liberal education achieved its strongest formulation. Gradually, but only gradually and by no means uniformly, the position of the clergy improved over the next fifty or sixty years, and the gain in respectability rubbed off on the dons. Some of the gain was in income, but some of it was social.

In the course of the second half of the eighteenth century and continuing into the early decades of the nineteenth century the financial position of the lesser clergy, to include the depressed curates, visibly improved, although the latter remained dependent upon the generosity of either the beneficed clergy or the patrons of clerical livings, whomever they might be: the crown, ecclesiastical bodies, the universities, or lay improprietors. The greatest assist to the impecunious curate came with the acts of 1813 and 1817 which established a minimum income of £80 per annum—not a certain guarantee, but still a vast improvement over earlier times. This was still merely half the £150 per annum regarded as a rock-bottom income for a respectable clergyman in 1816, and therefore inadequate unless the curate was fortunate enough to be holding down more than one cure.[1]

The beneficed clergy were better off, profiting from the extraordinary changes in the structure of farming that occurred in the second half of the eighteenth century and from the inflated prices paid for grain during the wars against France. More and more tithe payments were commuted from kind or leased, and the glebe was either farmed or rented at a good income. The beneficed clergy profited as well from augmentations to existing livings or from gratuities granted by patrons. The added income enabled the country clergyman to assume a style of life more in keeping with his richer neighbours from the gentry stratum. No historian would put the new parsonages of the nineteenth century on the same aesthetic footing as a splendid Tudor country house, or perhaps an odd Dutch-inspired

[1] R. B. Walker, 'Religious Changes in Cheshire, 1750–1850', in *Journal of Ecclesiastical History*, XVII (April, 1966), 79. Diana McClatchey, *Oxfordshire Clergy, 1777–1869* (Oxford, 1960), 75. See also W. R. Ward, 'The Tithe Question in England in the Early Nineteenth Century', *Journal of Ecclesiastical History*, XVI (April, 1965).

Jacobean manor; but whatever their failings, the new residences undoubtedly declare material prosperity.

In some periods, notably after 1780 or 1790, it is entirely conceivable that income followed rather than preceded the rise in clerical status. If this was indeed the case, it can be concluded that once the country parson had achieved greater prestige, it was found necessary to guarantee him the income essential to the style of a gentleman.

Undoubtedly, one of the most important reasons for the upward shift in clerical status was the entry into lower levels of the Church of new recruits, in this case younger sons of gentry. This would help explain the strong efforts made in the Regency period to augment the value of clerical livings, not only through such established measures as the use of the special fund called Queen Anne's Bounty, but also through the efforts of diocesan societies as well. Marriage into a higher rank of society is yet another example of how income may have followed status. The evidence for status mobility through marriage is as yet slim. It can be at least suggested that before 1750 parsons usually chose their wives from either labouring or farming families or from girls in domestic service, but that afterwards wives were increasingly selected from groups higher in the social scale.[1] A small number of clergymen married into noble or landed families, sometimes related but most often not, but the prevalence of this practice cannot at the moment be accurately determined.

The rise in clerical status between the mid-Georgian period and the end of the Napoleonic Wars is a very significant historical change. One indicator alone states the improvement in terms immediately recognizable to historians of England. In the 1750s country gentlemen still thought it entirely beneath their dignity to sit on the county bench with clerical JPs.[2] But in the early nineteenth century the clerical magistrate was a familiar sight, and this despite the fact that in 1774 the property qualification for JPs was increased two and one-half times from its former

---

[1] J. V. L. Casserley, 'Clerical Marriage in Anglican Experience', in *Celibacy: The Necessary Option* (New York, 1968), 88–9, suggests labouring and domestic families as sources for wives.

[2] I am indebted to Norma Landau for this reference from the Hardwicke Papers in the British Museum.

level. The parson of 1820 or 1830 was unquestionably a gentleman, on equal or near equal social terms with the squires of the neighbourhood, to whom, in fact, he might be related; and despite his income, which may have been barely adequate to his needs, undoubtedly superior in status to tradesmen, merchants, and the professional men of the country towns. According to some observers of the 1830s, an income of £60 per annum characterized the lowest level of the middle classes,[1] and it is quite clear that this bottom group was not highly regarded on the late Georgian ascription scale. Yet a clergyman of the same income in the same period was considered to be a person of worth and quality. And as he rose in status, so did the university don, to whom his fortunes were so closely related.

These were the long-run changes that resulted in the respectable clergymen of the late Georgian and early Victorian periods. But in the meantime, the improvements were not rapid enough to relieve the fellows of the colleges from the reproach of inferior birth and ill-breeding. Sensitive to the accusations, the collegiate fellowship attempted to mend their ways in order to improve their reputations. The easiest solution was simply to leave, and the majority of fellows did so. Having no specific teaching or administrative functions, they moved out of residence and went off to seek their fortunes elsewhere, some in London, some as tutors to great families, some as schoolmasters, to become active men of society. Those who remained behind tried to approximate the standard of life expected of a man of liberal education, spending the college income on comforts rather than on teaching. The revolution in the decorative arts that transformed London and the homes of the rich in the eighteenth century also changed Oxford and Cambridge, and the consequences of the new ethic of liberality remain to this day for all to enjoy. Gardens changed from Dutch or French to the new informality and ease associated with Capability Brown. Panelling went over medieval stone. Furniture, china, silver—all à la mode—were introduced. The college common room, a cross between a London dining club and the library of a country house, arrived—in short, the new, generous, breezy life style that accompanied an age of un-

[1] W. H. Mackinnon, *On the Rise, Progress and Present State of Public Opinion* (London, 1828), has a three-class model of social structure based on wealth or income.

precedented national prosperity. The institutional amenities so highly valued in the Georgian period and emulated long afterwards eased a number of problems facing the maligned college don and were also partial compensations for the inequities of income that divided the university community into arrogant haves and resentful have-nots.

The resident fellows made still other efforts to approximate the model of an educated man. Having accused one another of pedantry, they bought, sometimes collected, and even read the great modern works of literature and new editions of classical works indispensable to the liberal gentleman. They subscribed to literary periodicals and occasionally contributed to them. In several instances, they founded short-lived periodicals of their own. Suitable purchases were made for college libraries, and evidence exists to establish that books were borrowed in sizeable numbers and presumably read.

In her recent Bryce Memorial Lecture, Dame Lucy Sutherland has found other kind things to say about the Georgian universities.[1] It is certain that there was some renewed educational activity. Several chairs were founded, and new courses of lectures were given in both the arts and sciences. Undergraduates were sometimes encouraged to attend the new courses and the supplementary lectures.

Yet the new subjects were never an intrinsic part of the official teaching curriculum. The new lecture courses were more often private than official and were usually paid for by fees, a precarious means of support, rather than by university endowments. Some of the new instruction offered was not strictly speaking liberal, not part of a general education, but professional. One of the new professorships was the Vinerian Chair of Common Law which Blackstone held; and one of the subjects in which good teaching was still to be found was anatomy, although only the subordinate lecturers were competent in all that was left of a once splendid school of medicine.[2] A great deal was left to the initiative of undergraduates. Those who were especially interested in receiving an education could find the opportunity to do so, but

[1] Dame Lucy Sutherland, *The University of Oxford in the Eighteenth Century, A Reconsideration* (Oxford, 1973).

[2] H. M. Sinclair and A. H. T. Robb-Smith, *A Short History of Anatomical Teaching in Oxford* (Oxford, 1950).

it meant hiring private tutors to learn modern languages, or perhaps an exotic one, and to be instructed in music. Probably a considerable number of students showed this initiative, but we have no real way of knowing.

At Cambridge after the 1750s, it was apparent that mathematics had come into new prominence, rising up as an examination subject as the old scholastic disputations dragged on. But mathematics did not satisfy all the necessary criteria of liberal instruction. It was not a literary subject, and it was not humanistic—that is, it did not have much to do with interpersonal relations. Classical learning was not an official part of the studies leading to a degree, although the languages were certainly taught in the colleges. The greatest Greek scholar of the age was a Cambridge man, Richard Porson, but his value to undergraduates and colleagues was considerably less than it might have been. When elected to the chair of Greek in 1792, he chose to reside in London. How useful he would have been in Cambridge is problematical, for he was a man of strange habits and, unfortunately, an alcoholic.

In general, at Oxford and Cambridge new subjects grew up on the edges of the universities, the special interests of particular individuals, neither provided for by college and university endowments nor regularly scheduled. Here and there, notable scholars and scientists appeared, but few Oxbridge professors or dons enjoyed an international reputation or made significant contributions to scholarship. And because the dons and professors were anxious to make an appearance as men of the world, and because the traditional programme of studies was regarded as illiberal outside the universities, confidence in the education provided by the universities inevitably declined, and teaching, no matter what the level, was half-hearted. Indeed, professorial teaching virtually ceased.

The definition and purpose of a liberal education had altered in the course of the eighteenth century, and the universities did not keep pace. The new age demanded a character formation theory of education. To this, the universities could only answer that they had one, that their historic association with the Church of England and the superintendence of young men by distinguished representatives of the Establishment were adequate to assure the formation of a suitable moral character. But

Christian ethics and religious morality were not exactly what a secular age enamoured of pagan models and uninterested in the spiritual world wanted. To a century that self-consciously regarded itself as enlightened and placed a high value on the routine activities of everyday life, the Anglican conception of education for morality was narrow, dogmatic, and bigoted. The only theory sufficiently utilitarian for the age, sufficiently geared towards happiness and pleasure, was a theory that emphasized the cultivation of the whole man, the co-ordination of mind and body, the harmonious integration of all personal qualities in order to develop man's full humanity. No matter how strenuously clerical defenders of the universities argued that religion could not be divorced from the things of this world, that man's relationship to God was relevant to all conceptions of personal behaviour, Georgian critics remained unconvinced. Nor were eighteenth-century theologians more successful, for they too, overwhelmed by utilitarian thought and apologists for an Erastian Church, could offer no argument for the place of religion in education that did not merely underscore a wordly direction already fully accounted for in the courtier-gentleman ideal. As sin was a question of action or good works, introspection was largely unnecessary.

And so Oxford and Cambridge in the eighteenth century relinquished their leadership in education and lasted out the century in a peculiar schizophrenic state. The universities were composed of an odd mixture of melancholic monks and fashionable dons, of official old subjects and marginal new ones. A disparity was apparent between the official educational curriculum, with its leftover Aristotelianism, its disputations and scholastic exercises, and the style of life that had emerged as tangible proof of liberality and civility. As long as the means of education were not solidly joined to the ends, the task of civilizing the privileged members of English society could not be satisfactorily accomplished. As long as university education was conceived to be dysfunctional, there were bound to be difficulties teaching proper conduct to generations of undergraduates bringing with them to the universities a clearer idea of the correct uses of education than seemed to be offered in the official studies and teaching. In the long run, the university failure to connect means and ends in its educational curricula had profound consequences. Although the failure made impossible the pursuit of the foremost cultural purposes of the Georgian age and delayed university leadership in liberal education, in another age the disjunction between means and ends produced a remarkable educational efflorescence. But only because by then the Georgian theory of a liberal education had very nearly disappeared.

9

A Liberal Education in Practice:
George Robert Chinnery

IN THE eighteenth century a liberal education was given the immense burden of rendering men and women sociable, tolerant, and broad-minded in situations where also every encouragement was given to the pursuit of personal advantage. Ends were often in acute conflict with social practice. The result was an educational theory strikingly vulnerable, one that failed spectacularly to achieve its explicit purposes, and in fact contributed to its own difficulties.

Perhaps the inevitable end of any character formation theory is deep ambiguity. The theory must depend upon a total conception of society, and those who formulate it must have an anthropologist's understanding of culture. But the complexities of any culture elude the grasp of even the most rational and perceptive members of it. The rapid movement of modern history, the continual change in underlying social and economic conditions invariably defeat any attempt to derive a workable notion of character from society. No sooner is a particular character or type decided upon than the cultural conditions presupposed by it have changed.

Formation of character as an educational objective can perhaps only succeed where the role for which the individual is prepared is acting. Only the actor is able to cope with changing cultural conditions, for only he is truly adaptable or malleable, having no real identity of his own. It is a fascinating commentary on the Georgians, who were very much attracted to the theatre—and also enjoyed being painted in other guises, as Commodore Keppel assumed the pose of the Apollo Belvedere and the scandalous Lady Hamilton was turned into Nature—that they glimpsed this truth from time to time and were troubled by it. Here, for example, is the wonderfully perceptive portrait of Chatham drawn by his intellectual disciple, Lord Shelburne: 'It was the fashion to say that Mr. Pitt was violent, impetuous, romantick, a despiser of money, intrigue, and patronage, ignorant of the characters of men, and one who disregarded consequences. Nothing could be less just than the whole of this. . . . He certainly was above avarice, but as to everything else, he only repressed his desires and acted. . . . He had had a fine voice and very happy articulation. He passed his time studying words and expressions, always with a view to throw the responsibility of every measure upon some other, while he held a high pompous unmeaning language. Yet good as his parts were, he was afraid to trust to them, and was a complete artificial character. It gave him great advantage to serve a turn, by enabling him to change like lightning from one set of principles to another, for which to do him justice, he had an extraordinary quick eye. . . . What took much from his character was that he was always acting, always made up, and never natural, in a perpetual state of exertion, incapable of friendship, or of any act which tended to it, and constantly upon the watch, and never unbent. . . . He was very well bred, and preserved all the manners of the *vieille cour*, with a degree of pedantry however in his conversation, especially when he affected levity.'[1] The Georgians realized that in order for their educational theory to succeed they must all be actors. They also realized that acting was a corruption of the values they wanted to profess. For if, as Jane Austen reminded them, we only play roles, we come to believe in them and lose our moral insight. We are, in Shelburne's words, 'artificial characters', untrue, for only what is natural can be true. In their own estimation the chief vice of the Georgians was hypocrisy or, as they often called it to soften the pain, 'affectation'. 'As the mixt intercourse of ranks has promoted the refinement of our manners, and improved the Charms of Society,' wrote a young don who happened to be Jane Austen's brother, 'it must be owned that the consequent desire of pleasing our Friends, and a wish to become eminent in our little circle of acquaintance, has been sometimes produc-

[1] Lord Fitzmaurice, *The Life of William Earl of Shelburne*, I (London, 1912), 58–61.

tive of an over-strained behaviour, to which we have given the name of *Affectation.*'[1]

To this problem there was no obvious solution. Driven by an extraordinary moral imperative, possibly as grand an educational purpose as has ever been known, the Georgians had no choice but to attempt what was virtually an historic mission. Finally, the play was over, and the puppets were put away—a Victorian view, incidentally, of the frivolity and pretence of Georgian social behaviour. The eighteenth century was probably the last time in England's history that an effort was made by a culture generally to construct a holistic theory of education. Attempts were made by individuals in the following century to revive the theory, but they achieved only limited success under special conditions. Having learned from the previous age, nineteenth-century culture was by and large content with far less ambitious educational aims.

There is no better way of illustrating the many tensions caused by the ambiguities within the Georgian theory of a liberal education than by turning to an actual case study. A rare collection of materials enables us to reconstruct in microcosm Georgian society in its final years. It also enables us to recognize the anomalous position the universities occupied at the turn of the century, and to measure the effects produced on undergraduate conduct by the continuous tension between the university and society.

Preserved in the library of Christ Church, Oxford University, is a fourteen-volume correspondence between an undergraduate and his family, especially with his mother, from the beginning of 1806 to the end of 1811. The letters were exchanged nearly every day, and deal with the education, the personal problems, the home values, and college life of an undergraduate whose name was George Robert Chinnery.

Of the outward circumstances of the family, there is only a little information available. William, Chinnery's father, was one of the four Chief Clerks of the Treasury, a high-ranking position somewhat reduced in tenure by the reorganization of 1805. His salary was substantial, being perhaps £1,400 per annum; and while considerably less than that of a peer of the

---

[1] *Loiterer*, ibid., 5.

realm or a great City financier, it was on a par with one of the poorer episcopates of the Church of England or the income of a member of the middling gentry. William Chinnery was dismissed from the Treasury in 1812, not too long after his son left the university.[1] While at Christ Church, young Chinnery showed signs of being interested in a law career. He may in fact have entered his name at Lincoln's Inn, but there is no indication that he was called to the bar or even read law. Actually, he followed his father into the Treasury. He became first an Assistant Clerk of Revenue, at a much lower salary than his father had received; he was then made a private secretary to one of the junior secretaries. He left the Treasury in 1823 after a relatively short career. Nothing further is known of his circumstances.

The question of why Chinnery was sent to Oxford is puzzling if the Treasury lists are correct—and they certainly must be—in indicating his subsequent career in government. He followed in his father's footsteps, clearly using the path the family had prepared. The mathematical training he received at Oxford could have been privately obtained. Residence there could easily be considered a superfluous expense, for if it was merely the 'interest' of a great person the Chinnerys hoped to attract, they already seemed to enjoy it. By the standards of the day, they were remarkably well connected. H.R.H. the Duke of Cambridge was a friend of the family. Members of the titled nobility were included in their range of acquaintances. Chinnery's father appeared to have no difficulty in paying out the huge sum of £300 per annum for his son's Oxford education, an amount three times the minimum cost. A generous margin for extras and entertainments was obviously included. The solution to the puzzle as to why George was sent to Oxford lies, in fact, in the words Mrs. Chinnery composed for her son to recite to the great Dean Jackson of Christ Church: 'I have neither high birth, nor splendid connections, nor wealth to inherit, upon which I might rely,—my advancement in life must rest wholly with myself and be the effect of my own labours.'[2] In context, this was true. Oxford was back-up or insurance for Chinnery in

[1] Biographical details are from *Alumni Oxoniensis* and J. C. Sainty, *Treasury Officials, 1660–1870* (London, 1972).
[2] Chinnery Papers, 10 May 1811.

case his father's influence at the Treasury failed. Positions won by patronage could be lost in the same way. There was always an element of worry connected with launching a son into a career. The scramble for place was close, and the requirements for acceptance into the best London social circles were high. Families of good income, accustomed to being seen in fashionable places yet occupying a relatively poor hereditary estate, were particularly anxious about the future welfare of their sons. Fathers (and mothers) were careful to explore all avenues of possible success. Merit—the 'stock of fame' to which Mrs. Chinnery referred in one of her key letters—could not be totally discounted even in an age of patronage. Chinnery was sent to Christ Church, the leading Oxford college of his day, as Trinity was at Cambridge, because Jackson was reputed to be an influential and well-connected churchman, whose voice reached to the royal court and to Westminster. He came to widen his career choices by widening the circle of interest that could be mobilized in his behalf.

He also came to Oxford to learn how to conduct himself in public. He had grown up in the sheltered environment of the country. At one time, the Chinnerys had lived in Marylebone, although a good three decades before Beau Nash developed Regent's Park into the picturesque terraces and villas we find there today. When he was young, his mother insisted, against the advice of friends, on raising him even further away from the centre of the city. London's unique excitement was beginning to pall in the 1790s. The increasing congestion, rioting, and spread of political radicalism made the capital less urbane, less civilized, less stimulating than it had appeared to the earlier Augustan writers so closely connected with its rise. Mrs. Chinnery found the city vile and corrupting and retreated into the garden of Epicurus. She settled her family within commuting distance of Whitehall. But the time had come for George to enter the great world and to experience the rites of passage of a university education. Tutors could only take a young person's education so far; at a certain point, he had to have a 'public' education.

When Chinnery matriculated at Oxford, he was merely sixteen years old. His age was untypical of that of entering undergraduates. The median age of entry had risen over the eighteenth century to about eighteen in 1808. Not only had George been protected in the country, but he was unusually young and immature. His mother had encouraged his immaturity by keeping him innocent. He had been raised a teetotaler in a hard-drinking age. He had grown up primarily in the company of women—his mother and a younger sister. The rowdy, undisciplined behaviour of aristocratic boys who had survived the experience of a Georgian public school was unfamiliar to him.

In the pages of the correspondence Mrs. Chinnery emerges in marvellously explicit colours. She was intelligent, driving, and neurotic. Because a career in public life was closed to women, she pinned her personal hopes on her son. Throughout the entire three years of their correspondence and while he was at home during the holidays, she never tired of reminding him, sometimes with astonishing acerbity, that his future was in his own hands, that he had a dazzling reputation to make, and that young men were sent to universities precisely to obtain fame. When she herself was not prodding him on, she instructed Chinnery's younger sister to keep the pressure up. His eventual triumph, he was informed by his mother, would vindicate her careful upbringing—indeed, advertize it, and bring to general notice her meticulous attention to the details of his education, her judicious selection of tutors, her incomparable domestic virtues, and her unparalleled maternal love. His failure, on the other hand, she was quick to say, would be entirely upon his own head, the consequence of his own indolence and negligence. She herself would be utterly blameless, although, of course, betrayed. 'Remember the Parable of the Talents,' she wrote to him during one exasperated moment. 'You will, not only in the next world, but even in this, be called upon for abilities equal to the care and extraordinary attention you have experienced. You ought to be the cleverest man of your time; . . . you have been watched with very *un*common care!—If you do not rise to the height where the world expects to see you,—you will fall very low indeed!—Take care, my dear George,—*it will be a misfortune to you, to have been educated by me, if you are not the first man of the age in which you live!*'[1]

[1] Ibid., 19 February 1809.

Mrs. Chinnery was voluble, over-educated, and frustrated by the paucity of suitable outlets for her own abilities. The signs of her frustration are obvious. She succumbed periodically to severe headaches, brought on by a continual, fearful anxiety for the daily and future welfare of her revered child. Her possession of him was extraordinary. 'You can form no idea how I love you! —nor can you ever, for even a father's is not equal to a mother's love!'[1] She asserted in the most alarming oedipal terms that her son had no right to an independent life, that his body belonged to her, and that he could not in any way neglect it without harming her. 'What I have therefore to request is that you would regard your person *as mine*, and as something inestimably dear to me, and take care of it *as such*.'[2] The advice she gave him—to jump sideways over a ditch rather than frontwards, as less likely to cause injury—could only have been psychologically damaging, encouraging the dependence begun in the home. Under his mother's matriarchal authority, Chinnery used his letters to confess himself, to purge away his guilt, and cleanse his trivial sins.

In order to realize his mother's ambitions for him, Chinnery was exhorted and commanded to work hard at his studies. He was told to obey his tutors, perform all assignments, and in general seek the counsel of senior men of reputation. This seemed simple advice, but it was difficult to follow. The great Dean was aging and capricious, withdrawing or granting audiences as they suited him. Chinnery's official college tutor was overworked, due to a typical Georgian structural deficiency in the distribution of teaching assignments, most collegiate fellows having nothing to do and a few having too much. George was consequently assigned to a private tutor; and this man, a future bishop, but in 1808 young, unknown, and inexperienced, his own prospects dependent on clerical patronage (of which the Chinnerys had none), did not always show tact and understanding in dealing with a socially immature, naive, and protected young man. Furthermore, the House, in common with several leading Oxford and Cambridge colleges, was groping its way towards new teaching schedules and assignments in a slow but steady effort to raise the standard of achievement for serious young men. The mixture of confused aims, of old

[1] Ibid., 19 June 1808.
[2] Ibid., 19 January 1808.

practices and innovations, of competing social values, added immeasurably to the tension Chinnery experienced. The authorities of Christ Church did not appreciate the impact of the contradictions of the period. Nor did they perceive how study habits were upset by such traditional privileges as allowing senior students to appropriate the rooms of freshmen at virtually a moment's notice at the commencement of each new term.

Chinnery was instructed by his mother to put up with all these inconveniences and disruptions and to steady himself for a dazzling university career. By excelling in his studies, she reasoned, by composing and delivering impressive declamations in Hall, by achieving a superior performance in the university examinations, he would, she was confident, attract the attention of his teachers, make the old Dean smile, be noticed by some scion of good family, and catapult to fame.

Chinnery accepted his mother's advice, and wrote faithfully to her of his efforts to comply with her standards. He sent her work schedules and complied with her criticism of his themes and declamations. He watched his spelling and tried to improve his penmanship. But almost from the outset her magic seemed to fail. The view of the world with which he had been raised seemed hopelessly inconsistent with what he found in Christ Church. His honesty, his diligence, and his earnestness were applauded by his mother but laughed at by his peers and barely acknowledged by his teachers. His general innocence stirred no one's approval, and the bullying he received hardly anyone's compassion. Despite the well-publicized changes in the curriculum and the tightening of university discipline over undergraduates, it was apparent that all students were not treated equally by university authorities. Mrs. Chinnery's anger increased in direct proportion to her anxieties. She began to accuse the college authorities of playing favourites, of chasing bluebloods, of failing to maintain adequate standards of conduct, and of permitting, either by neglect or complicity, dissolute habits of behaviour. Mrs. Chinnery's reproaches, directed towards Christ Church, were also displaced on to her son. She feared he was being seduced into another kind of life and was being torn away from her influence. She was furious because Oxford was an essential part of her plan to launch her son into a fashionable career. She had bent all her resources and energies towards this object for sixteen years, to the neglect, as she admitted, of Chinnery's younger sister, and now all her schemes and calculations seemed a receding bough of Tantalus. She claimed that Oxford was a mistake and that she had been misled by its reputation as a place of learning. Had she known the true situation, she exclaimed in desperation, she would not have sent her only son to be corrupted there. In view of her ambition, however, her protests are totally unconvincing.

Mrs. Chinnery knew very well what the realities of late Georgian cultural life were. She had hoped that her son would be able to withstand the temptations and vices of undergraduate social life through her careful upbringing. She spared him a public school education until he was old enough to brace himself against the wasteful extravagance and incidental violence of a residential, educational institution. She had carefully restricted her instruction to precisely those ideals and values which placed the world of affairs in a favourable perspective. She had directed her education to only one part of Georgian liberal education—to the need for self-restraint, to the necessity of virtuous conduct, to truthfulness and modesty. She did not tell her son that there was another side to getting on, for which, unfortunately, values of another kind were required. She began to see, however, that unless she told George the realities of his situation, he was not likely to achieve either success or reputation.

In the beginning she played for time, hopeful that the insults and teasing her son received were no more serious than simple initiation rites. But soon her advice to him became contradictory, and she realized how confused he must be. Finally, she implicitly admitted that George was ill-equipped to cope with Oxford, and that she would have to correct the deficiencies of a one-sided upbringing. A new period of parental guidance now opened up to ease a perplexed adolescent into the world of gossip, intrigue, and favouritism.

Mrs. Chinnery encouraged—it would be more accurate to say ordered—her son to be sociable. The policy of high-minded withdrawal was a disaster. He would never make friends. George showed a tendency to turn his thoughts inward and retreat from his bullying companions. He read French novels and identified with the young protagonists. She would have none of it and insisted that priorities be kept firmly in view. In the beginning, she admitted that it might take time for George to acquire the requisite social airs—'You must have a greater experience of society before you venture too far.' But at the same time, she introduced him to the arts of dissimulation. He needed, she wrote, 'something to make you seem pleased with the society you are in, I would have you say and look;—something, to give you an appearance of greater animation.'[1] If Chinnery were well liked, she reasoned, he would make friends and meet the right persons. She reproached him far more for infractions of the rules of sociability than she did for errors in phrasing or grammar. While telling him always to be true to himself—and it would thereby follow that he could not be false to any man—she told him at the same time to conceal his true feelings, to dissemble his true nature, and to be one of the crowd. He was 'to wear the mask of gaity and indifference'.[2] He was to play the philistine. The problem of drinking inevitably arose. An acute moral crisis in the Chinnery household followed, as George had always been too young to drink. In the beginning, she told him to inform his hosts that drinking 'leads to a chest inflammation, and his father has forbidden it.'[3] But this ruse convinced no one. Evening 'wines' were a sacred tradition in Oxford, and students had to attend them daily, taking turns at being host. The man who does not drink, undergraduates told him, must be a spy for the college authorities. But a little wine and George was very nearly under the table, to the amusement of his peers. A dilemma, but solved. He was to stroll through the evening with a glass in hand, taking imaginary sips and acting a little merry. Friends were necessary, and he must go to nearly any length to obtain them. 'You will recollect that I never wished you to deprive yourself either of *exercise* or *society*,' she wrote to him. '[O]n the contrary, I have told you that *health*, without which nothing can be done, depends on the former,—and that the latter, even of a bad sort, may be more useful to you than books, because experience of all sorts of men, and all sorts of things, is very desirable at your age. For instance during all this week [the end of term] I should think it stupid and absurd were you not to take the full enjoyment of the gaity of

[1] Ibid., 15 February 1808.
[2] Ibid., 20 January 1808.
[3] Ibid.

Oxford; and prefer *that* to study, except in as much as you must prepare for Collections. Give all the rest of your time up to Society,—see every thing, join in every thing, and be all that your youth should make you be,—gay, animated, and curious about every thing that is going on.'[1]

Above all, Mrs. Chinnery wanted George to be popular. Do 'they all really despise you,' she inquired, 'or ... [do] they esteem your character & are themselves vulgar liars. Pray explain yourself a little more,—hang all the Greek & Mathematics,—the first thing is to know how to make yourself respected.[2] She lectured him on the importance of role-playing, told him how one man must learn to play many parts, or 'vary his character as the cameleon,' for this was the 'fiery ordeal [he] must encounter on the great theatre of the world.'[3] She mentioned Garrick, confusing the theatre with real life (which in fact was Garrick's purpose), and she used acting as a model for the kind of public conduct she could no longer avoid telling him about. Having raised him to be honest, worthy, straightforward, and earnest, she now suddenly reversed herself and told him to be realistic, to hide the truth about himself from his circle of peers, and to pretend to adopt their way of life. She recommended 'a principle to you to which I hope you will attend through life,—and that is, *never to risk any thing in public*. Whether it be an examination, or a declaration of your sentiments, or an act of much less importance than either.'[4] He can be different, she said, but he was not to *affect* being different—a fine distinction and a fine line to walk. Finally, to cap the fundamental contradictions to which poor George's Christ Church career had given rise, she warned him in the loftiest terms to watch out for deceitful flattery: this, she said, was the greatest of all vices. Clearly the game was to deceive others but to avoid being deceived oneself. It is hard to avoid moralizing: the person who dissembles because he knows social values require it will also know that others must be dissembling, too. Or, to use the words of a Georgian who very well understood the ironies of his culture, 'Every man . . . may, by examin-

[1] Ibid., 22 June 1808.
[2] Ibid., 17 June 1808.
[3] Ibid., 31 May 1808; 15 June 1808; 26 January 1809.
[4] Ibid., 27 April 1809.

ing his own mind, guess what passes in the minds of others: when you feel that your own gaity is counterfeit, it may justly lead you to suspect that of your companions not to be sincere.'[1]

Elsewhere in the correspondence, Mrs. Chinnery completes the strategy for being sociable. She gives her son advice on how to make an agreeable impression, how to walk, to incline his head when speaking to a lady, and to acquire the 'gentleness and politeness of a well-bred gentleman'. As his body is rather stiff, she supports his decision to take fencing lessons. Somehow, he must develop a livelier personality. She hopes he will learn to be expressive and to be able to speak in public, and to this end she consents to let him participate in the debating societies then springing up in Oxford, although half of them were an excuse for tippling. Above all, sociability is to be achieved by learning to converse well, with the appropriate body gestures, for of all accomplishments, she said, conversing was the most fascinating. Here, at last, she was able to draw upon one of the nobler Georgian sentiments, after having spent so much anxious time instructing him how to conceal his feelings. In conversation he was to do all he could to enable others to talk freely, to bring them out, and to put them at ease. This was one of the most valuable arts he could acquire, she explained. Besides, what better way to become popular than by this civilized manner of flattery!

At one level, there is nothing particularly unusual or even historical about the Chinnery situation. It is natural for a young person living away from home for the first time to desire and seek friends, especially if his upbringing has been closely superintended. It is even more natural to desire friends in an educational setting which is communal, where residence is an essential part of the educational process, and where the notion of a fellowship or community is reinforced by tradition, ritual, and symbol. But at another level, Chinnery's experience is historical and temporal. Although in any communal situation there will always be some pressure for conformity, we must consider the operation of other cultural values. Not every young person away from home is impelled by a relentless set of social values that puts public behaviour and appearance foremost and

[1] Samuel Johnson, *Rasselas* (New York, 1962), 38.

makes individualism suspect. When high standards of personal conduct regarded as appropriate for the family collide with social values recognized as essential to success, the result can only be psychological confusion.

Chinnery's dilemma was undoubtedly his own, but it was also the dilemma of late Georgian England. Loosened standards of Taste, increasing cultural experimentation, and a greater latitude in child-raising were producing more independent-minded people. Mrs. Chinnery's highly personal correspondence with her son is certainly evidence of a changing cultural situation. Her letters are utterly different from the stereotyped advice from a parent to a son prevalent fifty years earlier. Lord Chatham's letters to his nephew at Cambridge, Lord Camelford, written in the 1750s (although not published until much later), are filled with the usual conventions of the courtesy book genre. The tone is impersonal and the advice universal.

In the early nineteenth century, young persons like George Chinnery were being raised to believe that merit would be rewarded, only to find the reality somewhat different. Because career opportunities for certain ambitious groups were still relatively restricted and the best jobs distributed by a few well-placed persons, greater frustration was being experienced. Every possible success opportunity was being explored by anxious parents high enough on the social scale to feel the necessity to keep up appearances, yet just a little too low to be assured that it was possible. When the universities appeared to revive in the early nineteenth century, parents once again started sending sons to them. Their continued worries are evident in the dissatisfaction expressed over the arrangements for teaching and the alacrity with which private teachers were hired. Of course, private teachers were hardly new, but there was a change in the purposes for which hired tutors were employed. In the eighteenth century, the reduction of the scholastic disputations to humorous pantomimes left room for varied reading for students wishing it. Parents corresponded with college tutors and recommended books, or they arranged for additional private teaching. Mrs. Chinnery was so concerned about the progress of her son that she wished to do the same, but the Christ Church of the early nineteenth century resisted what had once been acceptable parental overseeing or collaboration.

A Liberal Education in Practice: George Robert Chinnery

The formidable Dean Jackson did not like parents choosing private tutors for their sons—he arrogated this decision to himself. The Chinnery correspondence gives an amusing picture of Mrs. Chinnery attempting to insinuate George's old domestic tutors into the university in defiance of Jackson. The language and mathematics tutors, in desperate need of employment now that their protégé was away from home, behaved as if they were about to make a sneak attack on Oxford. The venerable 'big-wig' (as Jackson and other elderly heads were called in undergraduate patois) also issued a *ukase* forbidding parental visits during term as an instance of outside interference in the internal affairs of the House. Oxford and Cambridge were acquiring a special pride in their academic competence and did not wish to have their authority in educational questions challenged. Mrs. Chinnery had to be content—of course she was not—with exercising her influence through the letters she wrote her son.

In the Georgian period the pressure of getting along with others in order to get on was so great as to make conduct self-consciously painful. The requirement of being natural, pleasing, and unaffected for people who at the same time suspected others of deceit and hypocrisy produced an unavoidable tension in all social relationships, resulting in that 'over-strained' behaviour leading to affectation deplored by the writer quoted earlier. In cultural terms, this was the Georgian problem, and the resolution of it was not Georgian, but Victorian. In a later period, a liberal education did not have to produce 'actors' and 'artificial characters' because getting-on was no longer a matter of making unwelcome friends.

The central ironies of Georgian sociability are contained in the Chinnery experience. The ironies are exacerbated because the pressures for success in the world were becoming even greater as all the fundamental ambiguities of the earlier period continued. As long as liberal education was a character formation theory, there were likely to remain contradictions in behaviour and unforeseen cultural dilemmas. Intended to clarify the direction of moral change and to improve the whole standard of conduct, the Georgian idea of a liberal education succeeded finally in complicating everyday behaviour. It is no surprise that civility fell short of achieving its historical mission. From the start, it had been too open-ended to shoulder the cultural burden placed upon it. It is also no surprise that hypocrisy and affectation were two of the most common ethical terms in the eighteenth-century vocabulary. This is perfectly understandable in light of the meaning of a liberal education.

George Chinnery disappeared from view and from history after leaving Oxford. The ultimate effect of his upbringing and education are for us impossible to assess. Some of the evidence suggests that, after all, he coped surprisingly well with the outrageous pressures he encountered in the tug of war between home and university. He excelled in his studies, triumphed over his tutors who teased him as much as they taught him, and followed his father into the Treasury. Perhaps this alone was a vindication of the persistent attention he received from Mrs. Chinnery during his formative years. Yet in the larger sense— the sense that meant most to her—she failed. George Chinnery never achieved the 'stock of fame' or the place in history for which his mother tenaciously prepared him. How she took this we shall never unfortunately know.

10

The End of the Georgian Theory of a Liberal Education

THE THEORY of a liberal education assumed that Georgian culture was static; otherwise, there would have been no possibility of developing conduct along the lines of universal principles. Relative standards of behaviour, for reasons we have been discussing, were too threatening. Yet English society in the eighteenth century was not static; it was dynamic. And it was because of the gap between a dynamic society and a static theory that the ambivalence we have noted arose. A society and a culture, however, can sustain ambivalence provided no crisis explodes working assumptions and commonplaces of thought. We have seen how the challenge of private feelings and personal experience was brilliantly contained within Georgian society and rendered safe. Yet a crisis did occur to disrupt the society and release the subtle changes in values that had been accumulating throughout the second half of the eighteenth century. Two decades of terrible war on a scale unknown in Europe since at least the seventeenth century threatened the basic security of the kingdom and the legitimacy of its social and political institutions. Although the dissemination of revolutionary ideas began with the revolt of the American colonies, it was actually the French Revolution that most affected the applicability of Georgian ideals to liberal education. The export to England of unsettling ideas, political, social, and more threateningly secularist than eighteenth-century England had known—perhaps it is more correct to say 'acknowledged'—interrupted the general concern with polite behaviour. Religion, which had ceased to play either a serious or a distinct role in the formulation of concepts of liberal education, gradually reasserted its influence in teaching and discipline.

The evangelical movement, which, considering its Wesleyan origins, already had a long history by the time the French Revolution began, made its appearance in the universities only after 1800, stimulating other branches of Anglican thought. Slowly, the religious reformation spread throughout the ancient universities and into the public schools, once again a factor in determining character and self-restraint.

The romantic individualism which had been slowly generating during the last decades of the eighteenth century now came fully into the open, creating a multitude of challenges to both the society and its view of an educated man. The whole civilizing ideal of the Age of Reason, to which humanist and courtier elements had been attached, was no longer the pressing cultural concern of the society. The improvement in manners, the delicate adjustments in personal conduct, the values of sociability and liberality, did not go entirely out of fashion. But they did begin to lose their moral urgency and educational supremacy in the face of more formidable problems.

The events of the French Revolution and the revival of political radicalism at home permanently disrupted the unity of the Georgian conception of a liberal education and eventually replaced what had been an integrated theory of human development with a variety of competing programmes and ideas. But if some of these borrowed components of the older theory, none of them could be happily recombined. The conceptions that came closest to integrating personality with society were Utopian theories of character formation, such as Robert Owen put forward, but these were tied to a particular course of social reconstruction.

A sustained attack was begun on the hedonism of the Georgian theory, on its pleasure principle and elements of self-interest, which were now aggressively associated with the conduct of a landed aristocracy. Self-interest should be replaced by self-sacrifice, said the reformers and radicals, and more attention should be paid to the condition of England than to manners. A society in the process of revolutionary change needs leaders equipped to cope with problems of change—this, too, was an attack on the Georgian tendency to confuse political leadership with society life. Quite possibly the greatest effect of the social dislocation of the early years of the nineteenth century on the inherited theory of a liberal education was in the permanent separation of means from ends. Henceforth, only non-liberal forms of education were to exhibit a direct connection between the means of education and the ends to which they were put, 'mechanical' or vocational forms of instruction, or, occasionally, professional education. But in neither case was the concept of the total man incorporated.

One unforeseen consequence of the era of revolutions was the restoration of Oxford and Cambridge to national prominence, and eventually to national leadership in education. In view of the distaste in which so much of university education had been held so long, this was a startling and unpredictable development. It must be said that university change was not entirely a matter of conscious choice but also of new conditions, new problems, and new values. Before the universities could adequately absorb liberal education ideals into their official curriculum, as they were trying to incorporate the requisite life style, historical conditions changed, and they were no longer as vulnerable to the original charges as they once had been. Instead of having to make a further effort at reconciling the disparities within a liberal education, the dons introduced changes in their education more in keeping with traditions they had ceased to revere but had somehow retained.

At the very beginning of the nineteenth century, while Chinnery was at Oxford, there began an historic change in the educational structure of the university which had momentous consequences for the subsequent history of higher education in England. It was also a change that half a century later produced an equally significant alteration in the character of public administration. Strictly speaking, the change began first at Cambridge in the second half of the eighteenth century; but because it occurred slowly and undramatically, its ramifications were not appreciated until Oxford followed the Cambridge example by enacting the famous Examination Statute of 1801.

The historic change was the establishment of the system of competitive and written examinations, accompanied by the corollary value change of the idea of the career through merit, or, as it was in the first instance, the idea of the reward for academic achievement. The precise cultural origins of both the Cambridge tripos and the Oxford examination system are essentially obscure, but enough is known of the social and institutional context of their early nineteenth-century development to justify a number of conclusions.[1]

It is certain that the development of modern examinations at Oxford and Cambridge owed only a little to the persistent eighteenth-century criticism of their methods of teaching and illiberal environment, for in general examinations played no part in either the selection or the education of the cortegiano. Examinations, degrees, systematic courses of study were all part of the educational machinery of the medieval university. Quite possibly, however, the question of career was mildly involved, although only in an indirect way.

By the end of the eighteenth century, changes in recruitment methods were occurring at certain levels of the aristocratic State. A few sinecures were eliminated under Shelburne, and his example was followed by the Younger Pitt. In several departments of government—notably, the Admiralty, the Plantation Office, and the Board of Customs—various efforts were made to recognize or reward competence and to keep politics out of some phases of their daily operations. At the Board of Trade under Charles Jenkinson, there was some talk of recruiting young men of mathematical proficiency, and a mini-cult of efficiency did establish itself in pockets of the universities during the wars against Napoleon. In Christ Church, where Pitt had been, and where the legendary Dean Jackson held court until 1810, there was certainly discussion about the need to prepare young men of mathematical proficiency for positions in government. But at no time was there ever systematic preparation of undergraduates for careers of that kind. In the Church the higher ranks remained closed, probably more closed in 1800 than earlier. And in both Church and State patronage, sponsorship, and 'interest' still predominated in selection. Making friends and being sociable were still indispensable for the ambitious undergraduate lacking high family connections. Yet there was an interim development. Success in the examinations, or making a name generally, was becoming a winnowing process, a means of attracting attention so that the appropriate social introductions might follow. Also,

[1] For a detailed discussion see Sheldon Rothblatt, 'The Student Subculture and the Examination System in Early 19th Century Oxbridge', in *The University in Society*, I, ed. Lawrence Stone (Princeton, 1974).

the university examinations were becoming one way in which candidates for college fellowships were selected. Chinnery felt this pressure acutely, but it was also felt by the sons of clergy, the largest single group of undergraduates at either Oxford or Cambridge. For them, a college fellowship was the first step towards a clerical career of their own or a financial assist through the early stages of a post-university position in law, medicine, or politics.

The new examinations, bringing with them a new spirit of work and, within limits, of competition, were related to the arrival of a different kind of undergraduate, in some respects but hardly in all like Chinnery. The change cannot in any way be traced to changes in the social class composition of the university. It was, rather, a generational and a cultural change. Scattered evidence from the last decades of the eighteenth century indicates greater parental concern for the education of children and closer personal supervision of their upbringing. This was one consequence of the changing view of servants. Filled with ideas of their self-importance and prodded on by ambitious and anxious parents, more studious undergraduates began to enter the universities, more inquiring, bolder in thought, and more inclined to independent opinions. They were also far more interested in controversial political and religious issues than their predecessors. It was a simple matter for polemical ideas to find their way on to the agendas of student debating societies or for dangerous ideas to pass into the rooms of students acquiring a distaste for the conventions of acceptable conduct and developing a commitment to romantic notions of personal liberty and self-fulfilment. By no means were all undergraduates intellectually and socially adventurous, but enough of them were to give Regency Oxbridge a distinct tone.

The new undergraduate was a formidable challenge to the disciplinary resources of the ancient universities. For a number of important reasons, some having to do with the indulgent propensities of *anciens régimes*, student discipline was not consistently enforced, and all public schools and most Oxbridge colleges were notorious for high living and dissipation—this was yet another reason why they were considered illiberal. But if drinking, gambling, brawling, and whoring were hardly consistent with civility, at least they were vices which university proctors understood. (And perhaps could justify. As some Georgian writers said, a polite society may have vice, but a barbarous one has crime.) Dons were not accustomed to students of more adventurous mind and less adventurous limb. Free-thinking among the elite youth of the kingdom was unsettling to the social peace. What was objectionable in a bachelor fellow was even more worrisome in a young man not yet arrived at maturity.

Unquestionably, however, university discipline was equal to the task of controlling a potential renegade or two. What made the situation truly complicated and difficult was the sudden and still largely unexplained increase in enrolments that commenced after the turn of the century and shot up sharply about 1810. Institutions accustomed to a long century of low matriculations and relatively small numbers of students now discovered them-selves confronting rapid rises. At the same time, the rate of student absenteeism during term time fell, so that there were not only more students, but they were in residence for a longer period. There was no question of the physical capacity of the universities to absorb greater numbers than they were accustomed to, although individual colleges experienced diffi-culties, but the swiftness of the increase, combined with the arrival of an intellectually bolder student, tested the structure of teaching and authority.

The new examinations were a response, then, if in the first instance an imperfect one, to these combined new challenges. They were an attempt to absorb student interest and, if possible, deflect it from subjects and activities more immediately threaten-ing to the surviving *ancien régime* in England. Examinations were also a means of engaging student leisure, of forcing students to spend their free time—of which there had always been too much in the eighteenth century—on matters of university and not personal interest.

None of these unprecedented changes removed the ambiguities of a Georgian and an Oxbridge education. They remained for several decades and were even intensified. The examinations and the new collegiate work ethic generally were driving the universities towards the notion of liberal education as intellectual discipline, in order, at least for a time, to keep undergraduates from being too much in the world, but at the same time raising the usual questions of pedantry and isolation. Undergraduates, uncertain whether examination success would help them find a position when they left the university, were still concerned with making friends and contacts. The sociability ethic developed in the eighteenth century emphasizing conversation, drink, and general merriment was still very much alive in the early nineteenth century, buttressed now by a cohesive peer culture unknown in earlier days. The strain on young undergraduates was further increased by romantic ideas of individuality and self-realization. Small wonder that we notice a worsening of all the cultural contradictions within the ancient universities as undergraduates were exposed to so many deeply conflicting values.

The ultimate result of the challenges and the university response to them was a development that halted whatever might have been an incipient movement to solve the troubling ambiguities of the Georgian theory of a liberal education. Instead of means and ends being united, the two were spread further apart. Parts of the ideal survived, but other parts failed to find a satisfactory embodiment.

For example, the principle of breadth or the general education feature was not really adhered to. To be sure, breadth must be understood in its proper Georgian context. It did not mean a wide-ranging choice of studies covering the major areas of knowledge, scientific as well as humanistic; for, as we have seen, whatever subject breadth a gentleman received in his education depended entirely upon the variety of classical writings to which he was exposed, with perhaps some modern authors and a little theology on the side. His reading in the classics could be extensive, or it could be limited to essentially the study of language. Breadth meant the total education a gentleman received—accomplishments of body as well as mind—and it meant that he was to remain an amateur or dilettante, that he was not to acquire a specialist or professional knowledge or skill, as Aristotle said when demonstrating that the freeman should not become too practised a musician, for then he would be like a slave, more interested in his skill than in his own improvement. Apuleius, repeating the great authority, saw no reason to be embarrassed because he could not play the flute like the famous musician Ismenias. And so the example and the principle echoed down the centuries to Georgian England.

The End of the Georgian Theory of a Liberal Education

Measured against this principle, the Regency universities were as deficient as their predecessors, and conceivably more so. While neither the colleges nor the universities had ever taken an interest in the recreations deemed essential to a gentleman, they had tried belatedly to introduce a little modern learning and fashionable Georgian texts, even though marginal to the main educational concerns. But once the new examinations with their competitive rankings took hold, whatever curricular *laissez-faire* existed was suppressed. College teaching was reorganized to prepare students for the ordeal of the new examinations. At Cambridge the tripos continued to be entirely an examination in mathematics until the foundation of a classics honours examination in the 1820s. At Oxford an initial attempt to create an examination containing a smattering of breadth failed, and by 1807 the curriculum had been settled in favour of narrow preparation and early specialization. Furthermore, scholastic logic—in Hallam's phrase, 'hostile to polite letters'—was revitalized, or, to quote the splenetic words of the Rector of Lincoln College, 'A violent affectation of Peripatetic learning has seized of late the fashionable college' and others were forced to follow.[1]

An exacting, and in the long run highly successful, study discipline was introduced. As this happened, the ancient universities were pushed towards principles of education quite at variance with the basic assumptions of the Georgian ideal. For competition is not sociability, nor is it civility and self-restraint. And the notion of a competitive examination is based entirely on the principle of testable knowledge, and not on a vague, broad understanding of the world or a general grasp of public affairs. The impulse in the early nineteenth century was towards the development of objective criteria for judging success, whereas in the unreformed universities of the eighteenth century objectivity was very nearly a reprehensible idea. Awards, honours, and recognition were not customarily based on objective criteria. They were granted largely for other reasons: privilege, rank, favouritism, nepotism, or to give one social group special assistance, as the sons of country curates and parsons were given scholarships to the universities to enable them to make contact

[1] W. R. Ward, *Victorian Oxford* (London, 1965), 15.

with the sons of prominent families. Objectivity was undoubtedly a departure from time-honoured principles, but it was also more than that. It was an attempt by the founders of the Oxford examination system and the examiners in both universities to reduce the possible areas of disagreement in the university curriculum. The general domestic crisis in England seemed to require an educational policy that put undergraduates to work without allowing them too much of an opportunity for free-wheeling discussions, at least not at the expense of the official curriculum. Within the first forty years of the nineteenth century the examination systems became progressively narrower in concentration and technical in nature and spirit. This was especially true of Cambridge, where the mathematical and classical honours examinations were very exacting and geared to problem-solving. In the course of time, written examinations replaced oral ones at both universities because of the large number of students to be examined, and because written examinations were or appeared to be far more objective. In both examinations the examiner became the major figure, and some form of cramming became the principal means of preparing for examinations. The college tutor himself was really a crammer—that is, if he understood his role properly.

By the 1830s, the selection of college fellows was tied to success in the examinations. Furthermore, to help ambitious undergraduates, a new system of private teaching was solidly installed in Oxford and Cambridge. While there had certainly been private teachers or coaches in the earlier decades and indeed well back into the eighteenth century, coaching had completely changed its character. In the past, private tutors, whether appointed by the families of students or selected by the colleges, provided either remedial instruction or a course of teaching more or less suited to the individual student. As university standards were low, it did not greatly matter whether a student read one book or another. But with the development of the historic modern examination system the prescribed curriculum had to be followed. Standardization of teaching was necessary. Private teachers now had the express purpose of preparing students for examinations. Their success in attracting undergraduates depended upon the number of successful (and highly successful) candidates they coached through the honours examinations.

The End of the Georgian Theory of a Liberal Education

All the major developments described above were not incompatible with improvements in the quality of both teaching and examining; but they had to be achieved at the price of those broader qualities of character attributable to education that came and went during the final days of the cortegiano ideal. Furthermore, to claim that the new kind of education and educational atmosphere encouraged 'polite' learning was unfortunately stretching the point.

As the university examinations system developed in the course of the first half of the nineteenth century, the emphasis in a liberal education shifted from the worldly social type who was its end product to what we now call proficiency, or the acquisition of skills. This was exactly what Aristotle and the Georgians said must not happen, for only slaves were proficient, but the outcome could not be avoided once the decision was made to restore examinations to the central position they occupied in the medieval university.

The skills or proficiency approach to education was deeply implied in what became for a long time the most important theoretical justification for a liberal education in the nineteenth century—the theories of cognition associated with the doctrines of faculty psychology. Faculty psychology has a very long pedigree in western civilization, a recognizable, if interrupted, history going back to classical Greece. Bacon wrote on the faculties of the mind in the seventeenth century, and later towards the end of it Jean Gailhard, who was concerned with the education of gentlemen, developed a complicated theory uniting a view of the function of mental faculties with humoral physiology, the latter taking him logically but somewhat freely into an analysis of the influence of climate, seasons of the year, and age on learning. As a pedagogical tool, Gailhard's theory can be called progressive in the sense that the child was being looked upon as a complex person, and not merely as a potential miscreant, although there was also a touch of that remaining in his theory. Gailhard urged the tutor to take pains to find out the effects of tempers and humours on learning ability, as 'It would be easie for him to remedy several inconveniences, whereof the causes would thus be known to him.'[1] Other writers of the same period

[1] Gailhard, 67.

referred loosely to cultivating parts of the brain, relying on horticultural images to carry the sense. Aubrey spoke of the mind being 'cultivated and improved and . . . understandings opened by good information of sciences, as the sweet rose-buds are opened by the morning dew.'[1]

Gailhard made an important, if conventional, theological distinction between body and soul, placing the mental faculties within the latter. He did not, however, insist on the complete separation of the two, for, in fact, his purpose in writing was to demonstrate the interconnection through physiology of mental and bodily functions. An anonymous pamphlet of 1736 indicates the survival into the eighteenth century of Gailhard's tradition when it begins, 'Soul and Body are the two constituent parts of man', but unlike Gailhard, the writer insists on the complete separation of spiritual and material elements. The soul, he says, 'is the cause of those several Operations, which we call *Perception, Understanding, Memory,* and *Will.*' The reason for maintaining the separation of soul from body in the early eighteenth century was to hold the materialists at bay. It was necessary to keep the thinking, judging, and acting parts of man securely in the spiritual dimension at a time when Locke's epistemological theories were becoming available. As the author of the pamphlet insisted, 'The Soul is so far from being necessarily *dependent* upon any material Powers, that it *commands* them all.'[2]

This criticism did not really shake the supporters of Lockean psychological theory, however, as the relationship of soul to body did not on the whole interest educational writers in an age of secular thought. In addition, it was no longer common, as it was in Gailhard's time, to use physiological arguments in connection with epistemology, although another science, physics, was certainly relevant. What did concern the Lockeans, however, was the neoplatonic revival of the later seventeenth century, which seemed capable of producing mischief equivalent to the belief in the supremacy of soul over the powers of mind. Here was a back door through which theology and the Church might make a surprise appearance. For the next one hundred and fifty years Lockeans, Hartleians, and sensationalists of

[1] Stephens, 140.
[2] *A Father's Advice to his Son* (London, 1736), 17–19. British Museum 1031.g.7(5).

various kinds fenced with upholders of doctrines of innate powers or inborn sentiments or common sense, and in this duel the theorems of faculty psychology were usually associated with the philosophical idealists and defenders of intuitive mental powers. Each school attempted to determine the ways in which environment did or did not influence learning ability. Throughout the eighteenth century disciplining the faculties or cultivating the mind were virtually universal expressions in any discussion of education; but the only systematic epistemological theory to hold the field was association psychology, or the school of Locke and Hartley. The two explanations for learning existed side by side. Only the philosophers worried about the difference. It is certainly possible to find in the early nineteenth century writers who will use both theories at exactly the same time without giving any hint of an inherent contradiction. In one breath they speak about the desirable associations that make up an education, and in the other they refer to parts of the brain that require massaging.

It is extremely difficult to ascertain what practical application either of these theories or doctrines may have had before 1800, since in the writings of so many authors references to them are hasty and careless. After 1800, however, a serious use of the theories becomes noticeable. Association psychology was, of course, the theory upon which John Stuart Mill's home education was based, the consequences of which he himself has traced in a fascinating autobiography. There was possibly some application of association psychology in the systems of popular education constructed by Bell and Lancaster in the early nineteenth century. But it is in connection with the doctrines of faculty psychology in particular that the history of higher education has to be written, for their influence, in conjunction with other cultural and institutional tendencies, was decisive.

In the first forty years of the nineteenth century, faculty psychology experienced a significant revival through the philosophy of Kant and the phrenological work of Gall and Spurzheim. Kant divided the faculties of the brain into two divisions, one containing the superior faculties, and the other the inferior. The principal task of education was to improve the inferior faculties in such a way as to aid the superior ones, as imagination, for example—a superior faculty in other schemes (and the one most discussed in Georgian theories of artistic creativity)—was to be cultivated to the advantage of understanding. Gall listed twenty-seven separate faculties of the brain and claimed to know their precise physiological locations. The importance of his work in the cortical localization of functions was that psychology was separated from epistemology and elevated in status, and that consequently neurological—that is, scientific—support was given to a body of thinking once highly philosophical or literary.[1] Even when the craze for phrenology was over in England in the 1840s (although not in America), and its scientific basis attacked, the metaphors and the goals remained.

It is obvious why cultivating the faculties was the single most important educational learning theory of the nineteenth century. The nineteenth century was the great age of the teacher. Numbers expanded enormously, teacher training became a branch of educational administration, teaching theories proliferated, and teacher associations were established to provide material and professional benefits. More than any other available epistmological theory, faculty psychology suited these developments, for only faculty psychology enhanced the teaching role. A comparison with the eighteenth century will make this clear. In the eighteenth century it could be said—and was said—that knowledge was available from books. Pressed to a logical conclusion, this meant there was little or no room for the teacher or that he played a subordinate part in learning. On the whole the teacher *qua* teacher was not held in high esteem in the eighteenth century. What prestige he enjoyed came from his status as a clergyman, and that status came late. Masters in private establishments were compared to tradesmen and put in the same category as music teachers, fencing masters, and the rest of the men who peddle 'accomplishments' in periods of new money and ambition. The private tutor in a gentle family had an ambiguous role, welcomed, if at all, as a clergyman and looked down upon as a tutor, a position perilously close to that of a servant. Even in Rousseauist theory, where the teacher appeared to be important, he was rather a stage manager than a director. His job was to facilitate in an unobtrusive way the child's own self-development.

[1] Immanuel Kant, *Education* (Ann Arbor, 1966), 70–1. See also Robert Young, *Mind, Brain and Adaptation in the Nineteenth Century* (New York, 1970).

The End of the Georgian Theory of a Liberal Education

The ideal teacher in the eighteenth century was not valued so much for his teaching as for his success in approximating Georgian models of virtuous and reasonable behaviour.

In the nineteenth century the teacher was important for scientific reasons. Only he disciplined minds; only he could determine which faculties needed strengthening, and, consequently, which programme of study was best suited to the student. It was his task to see that the faculties of mind were properly cultivated, that the will was strengthened, the judgement improved, the imagination warmed or excited, the reason developed, the understanding enlarged, or the moral powers exercised. The most important of all his teaching responsibilities was stimulating the memory. From this followed the heavy emphasis on rote learning, particularly in the lower levels of education. In time even the subjects that were taught became disciplines: tools for cultivating intellect and, reciprocally, instruments shaped by the mind. The spread of competitive examinations throughout society, from the universities to the schools to the civil service, the military, and the new professional organizations further increased the importance of the teacher and made his services indispensable.

It was in the language of faculty psychology that the great educational debates of the mid nineteenth century were conducted. The sentiment 'It is the sole business of the University to train the powers of the mind' resounds through the famous reports on Oxford and Cambridge produced in the 1850s and is heard for decades afterwards. The teachers of classical languages and literature unhesitatingly accepted mind-training as the basic goal of education and gave it precedence over refinement and elegance of expression. Anxious to preserve a teaching monopoly, they naturally argued that no other subject could discipline the intellect so uniquely or so effectively. Opponents argued to the contrary, offering special reasons why natural science or mathematical science or modern languages deserved equal ranking. Henry Halford Vaughan, the extraordinary personality who stands at the centre of the Oxford educational battles of the 1850s, even devised his own theory of faculty psychology with the assistance of scientific evidence produced by Hooker and Faraday. He maintained that the faculties of the mind were not perfectly formed at birth and that only by degrees or stages did the mind develop. Consequently, it was a mistake to introduce some subjects before the mind was prepared to receive them. Only those subjects especially suited to a particular phase of the mind's maturity were to be taught at that point. By reasoning in this way, he tried to postpone the teaching of classics until early adolescence. By arguing on empirical grounds, he hoped to prove that classics ought not to form the sole or even dominant part of a young person's education.[1]

Not only was there a battle of books during the discussions of mind-training, there was also a disagreement over which methods of teaching could best discipline the faculties. Was it true that lectures delivered by professors were inferior as mind-training to catechetical classes conducted by tutors because the former required the student to be merely passive while the latter forced him to actively participate in his own education? There were no final answers to a question that required neurological research to test the assumptions about faculty psychology; but, of course, there did not have to be answers if nearly all dons and schoolmasters accepted the premise that education existed primarily for purposes of training the intellect. It is only when we realize how wide-spread was the belief in the premises of faculty psychology that we understand why the Victorian 'humanists' like Matthew Arnold felt isolated and defeated.

Ultimately, there was no possible resolution to the battle of the books. New subjects began to develop so rapidly and the quantity of new information was so vast that the question of which subject could best cultivate a particular faculty seemed moot. Although in the past new faculties had always been created to take care of new subjects or methods, eventually the absurdity of this procedure was recognized.

A liberal education, then, was a matter of mind-training. The value of a particular subject or discipline lay in the number of faculties it could cultivate, so that classical languages could be said to stimulate the logical faculties, and especially the faculty of memory, classical poetry the imaginative ones, classical rhetoric the moral faculties, and so on. The old virtues—glory, nobility of mind, dignity, generosity, liberality—for which one

[1] E. G. W. Bill, *University Reform in Nineteenth-Century Oxford, A Study of Henry Halford Vaughan, 1811–1885* (Oxford, 1973), 231–6.

needed an exemplar slipped away, and cerebral qualities took their place. A change in education was made from social or socio-moral ends to intellectual means not directly related to those ends, and 'the minuter decencies and inferior duties' were sent packing.

'Vicious Poisons Lie Hidden Under
Sweet Honey'

THE THEORY of faculty psychology had the attractive justification of forcing students to work. This alone recommended it to
teachers in schools and universities, since discipline was indis-
putably a pre-requisite for learning anything. In the eighteenth
century dons and schoolmasters had not been successful in
compelling students more high-born than themselves to work
hard, and mental training appeared to be one solution to that
problem. Yet despite the success which made it the foremost
epistemological theory in England, for many teachers it failed
to exercise quite the same hold on the imagination as character
formation. The memory of a graceful, elegant courtier or the
gentleman of impeccable manners and faultless wit lingered on
in the nineteenth century and never quite vanished. Even those
more serious schoolmasters who rejected such frivolous, secular
models of behaviour were attracted to the idea that human
nature could be directly shaped by education. Such a view had
always been part of the education called liberal, and it was too
much to ask that teachers abandon it altogether. Accordingly,
there was a revival of interest in character formation from the
1820s onwards, beginning first in certain reformed public schools
and spreading in the next four decades to other schools and to
Oxford and Cambridge.

The most important reason for the revival of interest in
character formation was not the discovery or formulation of a
new central core of social values to which a type could be fitted,
as had been the case in the Georgian era. It was the very same
reason that made mental training the dominant psychological
learning theory of the nineteenth century. Character formation

thrust the teaching role into prominence and made the teacher an indispensable figure in education.

Before the teacher could acquire a dominant place, however, there had to be certain prime alterations in the Georgian theory of liberal education. Character for the Georgians, as poor Mrs. Chinnery finally confessed in exasperation, was formed in the world, and she correctly assumed that an aristocratic college like Christ Church, Oxford, was a microcosm of the world her son would someday inhabit. The more insulated, inward-looking school of the early and mid nineteenth century, however, was not a true mirror of the world. So the first change the nineteenth century had to make was the substitution of the teacher for the world as the permanent shaping influence on the personality.

A second change, certainly related to the first, was the development of a particular sub-culture, often an extension of the headmaster's own personality or values, to replace the general culture of the Georgian society. Whether a school or a college, this was characteristically a community within a larger community but with a strong sense of its relative separation, autonomy, and differences. A distinct feeling of moral or cultural superiority to the rest of society or to particular features of it—for example, industrialism—was a conspicuous element in the creation of a sub-culture. The school was one place, the world another. The public schools, certain select grammar schools, some newer Victorian secondary schools, and Oxbridge colleges were much more conscious of their power to influence personality through the manipulation of symbol and ritual in the nineteenth century than they had been in the eighteenth century, although it must also be said that the nineteenth-century student was much more willing to be influenced by the tone of his educational community than was his Georgian predecessor. In this regard it is significant to point out that the more aristocratic a Victorian school was and the more undergraduates expected to be independent and to be shaped only by the world at large, the more likely they were to resist efforts by schoolmasters to force them to subordinate their interests to the welfare of the institution. It took longer for Victorian character formation theories to penetrate Eton and Winchester, for example, than to take hold in Rugby, King Edward VI School, Birmingham, or Oundle. It is also pertinent to note that the influence exerted on the student to form his character in accordance with a particular institutional standard more often resulted in loyalty or affection (or violent antipathy) towards the school than in any observable alteration in his personality or perhaps values. But this is a difficult level of assessment, and we are, after all, presented with groups of disciples who professed to having been permanently influenced by their teacher or school.

A third point to observe in connection with the survival of character formation theories is the change in the ultimate values assigned to the end process. Whether we speak of Dr. Arnold or his followers, or experimental schools like Bedales, or the twentieth-century founder of the Outward Bound schools, it is not Georgian ideals that we find as the ends expected of liberal education. Victorian concepts of duty and social responsibility, or of self-sacrifice in the interests of national welfare, do not correspond to Georgian notions of civility and sociability, nor do late Victorian ideas of national—at times racial—superiority correspond to Georgian cosmopolitanism, or, at worst, Georgian condescension. Furthermore, the leadership ethic that took hold in the public schools and Oxford-Cambridge colleges, the cult of manliness that formed within them, was also a departure from past examples. For, as the Victorians never tired of saying, the person who assumed leadership in an industrial and democratic society had to be prepared to take a stand against the wishes of the majority. This was the meaning of the phrase 'a man of character'. It denoted a society without a consensus of values.

Within the older universities the interest in character formation made its strongest appearance in the middle of the nineteenth century. The reform of the fellowship system improved the teaching possibilities of the colleges. It produced a new type of career don who, like his counterpart in the leading secondary schools, was interested in making residence more attractive to undergraduates than it had been. For many decades, the don in his combination room and the undergraduate in his boating club did not meet except on levels of strained conduct. Friendship between teachers and students was unpredictable; and except for one or two colleges at each university, dons were neither receptive nor encouraging to undergraduates. This was bitterly resented.

In the 1860s, as part of the remarkable series of changes that transformed the ancient universities into their modern versions, dons set about systematically building trust and winning the confidence of undergraduates. Connected to this change was a fascinating youth cult. We hear the expressions 'Young Oxford' and 'Young Cambridge' and romantic talk of the renewing and regenerating power of a university experience for young and old alike. The impression derived from a reading of letters, essays, and biographies of the period is that for many of the new dons and professors the revival of the universities was tantamount to a religious and even a mystical rebirth. Feeding this development and keeping it alive until the beginning of the twentieth century was an aesthetic platonism of the kind to be found in the *Symposium*, a favourite reference for many classical dons, as well as public schoolmasters. The Oxbridge notion of a community of common purpose, where the only division is into senior members and junior members, also dates from this period.

Like the schools, the colleges turned inward, away from the world at large, although their announced policy was to bring Oxford and Cambridge back into the mainstream of national life. They meant this in a special way, however. They meant that it was their purpose to develop standards of values appropriate to changing conditions of social and political life. They would imbue their students with these values, so that in time, when the young men whom they educated left the universities for the world outside, they would bravely bear the Oxbridge message to the whole of society. But in the meantime, the process of education required the creation of a unique sub-culture within the universities, with a distinct tone, a recognizable style, and something of a social mystique.

It is this tone, style, or mystique that identifies Oxford and Cambridge and has continued to identify them until very recently. It was one direct result of the revival of interest in character formation theories of liberal education in the middle of the nineteenth century, although for support it drew heavily on the past association of the two senior universities with members of the clergy and the territorial aristocracy. The tone is so familiar—indeed, to some ears so reprehensible, permeated as it is with suggestions of social as well as educational superiority—that it is probably unnecessary to provide examples of its effect. But perhaps the tone will make a greater impact on the reader if examples are chosen to show how it affected individuals who were in different ways outsiders. To begin with, we have the impressions of a young Frenchman who visited Oxford briefly in 1895.

When Jacques Bardoux first arrived, he could not avoid drawing invidious comparisons between the intellectual life he experienced in Paris, where the spirit of the university spilled over into the cafés, and the schoolboyish presentation of the lectures he encountered in Oxford. He was repelled by the 'disjointed talk . . . nearly always . . . cold and colourless' of the professorial lectures he attended on Aristotle. The lecturer, he said, justified the study of Aristotle for 'practical' reasons. He thought this justification philistine. He was not surprised, therefore, that the undergraduates were devoid of intellectual commitment and lacking in curiosity. The quality of debate in the Union was weak and uninspiring, and he was bored until a fellow Frenchman carried the hour. 'The evening was a triumph for French thought, resplendent with ideas and genius.' He divided the undergraduates into three groups: the sporting types—ignorant but merry; the future parsons—virtuous and dull; the potential political and educational leaders—'less mature than our French students, they have read less and observed less.'

Having satisfied himself that French students and French university education were superior to English students and Oxford education, Bardoux was now free to enjoy himself, to fill in the background, and have a look at the overall setting. Suddenly his tone changed. The beauty of Oxford enthralled him, brought out his own youthful feelings and romantic impulses. It suggested to him that perhaps education consisted of more than the life of the mind, intellectual debate, and substantial learning, that simplicity of thought, perhaps even naïveté, had certain educational advantages. He was captivated by the sight of Shakespeare performed under a spring sky in the spacious gardens of St. John's, by the picturesque beauty of cricket flannels against closely-trimmed lawns—'These white forms running over the grass in the sunshine beneath the blue sky reminded one a little of the Greek athletes of old.' The women students floating over the grass in their *fin de siècle* clothes on their way to commems delighted him. In short, he, too, like countless foreigners who know only an urban university succumbed at last to the visual pleasures and quality of student social life, the rituals and traditions of Oxford, the sense of refinement and ease which he found. Feelings of superiority gave way to feelings of envy and nostalgia. And finally he saw, or thought he saw, the whole point of an Oxford education. Speaking of the best students, he said, 'If they have fewer ideas, they have more passions and more enthusiasms; if they are less prepared to meet objections, they have by way of compensation more convictions.' Noting the influence of the colleges, he wrote, 'They are more watched over than we are, and their conduct is stricter; if they are guilty of an escape [beyond the walls], they do not boast of it.' He was, of course, convinced that the French intelligentsia was better—no Oxford experience could shake him of that conviction—but his brief stay near the Isis had taught him to look for and value other qualities. 'There is no intellectual elite so strong as ours, but they undoubtedly have a political elite, and a much rarer thing, a moral elite.'[1]

These are, of course, merely the impressions of a charming and intelligent young Frenchman of good family. What is important, however, is not so much his personal opinions of the quality of Oxford teaching, although these are interesting, but the impact made upon him by the Oxford style. He does not appear to have been prepared for it, or if he was, undoubtedly wanted to be sceptical. But Oxford's aesthetic magic worked upon him, and though armed with Minerva's weapons, he was overcome.

We must listen to the description of another outsider, this time a prominent English Roman Catholic voice of 1869: 'Have the Catholics who wish to be associated with Oxford measured the spirit of the times, the freedom of thought, the irreverence of intellect, the mental pride, the impatience of authority, the independence of judgment in things the most sacred and august, the poison that exudes from every pore of the monster University, mixing itself in science, in literature, in society, pouring itself into the minds and the hearts, by its tenderness, its delicacy, its sensitiveness, its refinement, by its gentleness of manner, its

[1] Jacques Bardoux, *Memories of Oxford* (London, 1899), 9, 12, 13, 34, 35, 40.

charming address, its convincing reasoning, and embellished style—"Impia sub dulci melle venena latent?" [1]

In the 1860s the Roman Catholic hierarchy in England debated at great length the desirability of sending the flower of the Catholic youth to the ancient universities. By and large, the opponents won, having demonstrated how residence in an Oxbridge college could undermine Catholic orthodoxy even more easily than the advance of modern science, scholarship, and secularism. Free-thinking, agnosticism, modern science were all bad enough; but these were irresistible in the collegiate setting of young, beautiful Oxford. There was far less to fear from an examining, non-residential university like London. The notorious 'godless' students of Gower Street and the professorial teaching where many of the very same modern and progressive ideas were expressed did not dismay the Roman Catholic hierarchy, and Roman Catholics were not forbidden to take the examinations of the University of London.

Sociability, amiability, poise and style, sweetness and light: over and over again, these qualities and moods drift through the Victorian and Edwardian lives of men and women who went to Oxford and Cambridge. The tone was one against which the civic universities were always measured, against which they reacted, or to which they occasionally deferred. Their own contributions to the history of the English university were pioneering, and in many fields they led the way in promoting original research and scholarship. If they took some of their professors from Oxford and Cambridge, in return they gave some of their best minds to the Oxbridge professoriate. And yet, there was always that irritating tone, that suggestion of intrinsic superiority, and that enviable, generous environment. Undergraduates as well as academicians knew about it. The editors of the student magazine of Mason College, Birmingham (incidentally, the first man and woman team in university journalism in England) were apologetic because their publication lacked polish and literary style. Mason College had been founded as a scientific institution; and some students, sensing a technical tone to the magazine, asked for a style more suitable to the general reader.

[1] Vincent Alan McClelland, *English Roman Catholics and Higher Education, 1830–1903* (Oxford, 1973), 240–1.

'The difficulty which besets us', wrote one of them, 'seems to lie in the facts that, as students, most of us do not possess that real "culture" which . . . enables the Oxford and Cambridge undergraduates to write valuable and, at the same time, bright and readable articles for their reviews.'[1] In intellectual strength and seriousness their magazine unquestionably compared with the *Cambridge Review* of the same 1880s period, yet the sense of nagging inferiority was present, the absence of the indefinable 'real culture'. That the students of the new civic universities, drawn from the industrial and manufacturing districts around the leading cities, lacked sophistication and imagination was a charge that ungenerous Oxbridge visitors could level at them. The letters of the young literary critic Walter Raleigh, who went from Cambridge to deliver lectures at Owens College, Manchester, in March 1889, spurt with insult. He described his students as 'gaping loons' and 'mechanical dogs'. The professors did not even have 'the most distant approach to an idea of what culture is'. And the place as a whole, part of the new federated Victoria University, he called a 'vulgar, feeble body, and accordingly petty and jealous'.[2]

Comparisons between the Oxbridge style and the style of persons educated in other institutions could appear almost anywhere at any time, as in this memorandum from a high official of the Department of Education. Written in 1908, it was leaked to Parliament three years later, causing a sensation: 'The difference in respect to efficiency between ex-elementary teacher inspectors and those who have had a more liberal education [read Oxbridge] is very great. Very few of our inspectors have a good word to say for local inspectors of the former type, whereas those of the latter type are, with three exceptions, well spoken of. . . . [E]lementary teachers are as a rule uncultured and imperfectly educated, and . . . many, if not most of them are creatures of tradition and routine.'[3]

The Department of Education recruited heavily from Oxford

---

[1] *Mason College Magazine*, I, number 4 (April, 1883), 104.

[2] Lady Raleigh, ed., *The Letters of Sir Walter Raleigh (1879–1922)*, I (London, 1926), 120, 126–8.

[3] Gillian Sutherland, 'Administrators in Education after 1870; patronage, professionalism and expertise', in *Studies in the Growth of Nineteenth-Century Government*, ed. Gillian Sutherland (London, 1972), 283.

and Cambridge. It was also one of the last branches of government to abandon the patronage system of appointment in favour of civil service examinations, much as it had been the first administrative agency to enlist talented young men. The department was pleased with having anticipated the merit principle embodied in the Northcote-Trevelyan legislation of the 1850s and proud of the connection it had formed with Oxford and Cambridge, to whose glamorous recruits senior officials were partial. No doubt there is some truth in the harshly expressed opinion of the education received by many of the department's non-Oxbridge inspectors, but the phrases 'uncultured' and 'creatures of tradition and routine', while they may have a purely educational reference, struck contemporaries as yet another example of unwarranted class snobbery and social prejudice. It was easy to suspect that the labels were not thoughtful educational judgements at all, but preconceived ideas of appropriate social behaviour. It was because of the attractions of the Oxbridge style, the outward polish, poise, and social confidence that graduates of Oxford and Cambridge seemed to possess, that representatives of other universities, to include Scottish universities, insisted that the merit principle be strictly adhered to in all civil service appointments. Candidates from their institutions more than held their own on the written examinations for the Home Civil Service, even though the Oxford syllabus lent its students an advantage for certain periods of the nineteenth century. But the fear was that candidates would be eliminated if interviews were considered a major part of the selection process. The change in selection techniques after the first world war unfortunately confirmed the fear.[1]

The Oxford-Cambridge style, which was also related to the public school style—in fact, very likely was imported from those institutions—certainly rose in importance, or at least in publicity, after the reform of the universities in the middle of the nineteenth century. Young men preparing to enter the universities were aware of the style, expected to acquire it, and were, in fact, promised it. Biographies proclaimed the effect the environment had on the shaping of prominent alumni. Advertizements were

[1] R. K. Kelsall, 'Intellectual Merit and Higher Civil Service Recruitment: The Rise and Fall of an Idea', in *History, Sociology and Education*, History of Education Society (London, 1971).

sent out to the feeder schools—books, guides, pamphlets, essays, calendars, all in one way or another intimating that a particular style, a distinctive aplomb, was the inevitable result of residence in an Oxford or Cambridge college. 'Oxford will teach the graces which lend richness and interest to life, acquaintance with the great principles of literature and morality, respect of self and others, widened sympathies and admiration of human greatness.'[1] A few years at Oxford would provide 'an opportunity of gaining a tone in the society of well-bred and cultivated men'.[2] The famous proconsuls and bishops, the great headmasters and dons, well-known barristers and judges, and hearty country parsons repeated these sentiments as proof of the liberalizing education of the ancient universities.

Unquestionably the sweetness and light were there for those who went, remained, and absorbed the glamour and the romance, but was it liberal education? Doubtless, a thing is the name by which it is called. In their self-advertizement the collegiate fellowship certainly regarded the education provided in the universities as liberal, and they contrasted it with forms of education provided elsewhere—in technical schools, in vocational colleges, in the provincial universities. Yet what was the reality?

We return for a moment to the young visitor from France. What Bardoux saw had by and large occurred since the 1860s. The humanizing or liberalizing influences of the university were not the syllabus, not Aristotle, but the recreations and social life of the colleges: the balls, the games, the parties and picnics near the river, the performances of music and plays— Georgian sociability inevitably producing a man of liberal taste and generous inclinations. The moral influence of the university (if one could measure it, and Bardoux claimed to have done so) was also not in the syllabus, not a matter of reading and reflection, but a question of college rules and community sanctions, so that an adventure beyond the walls—a cause for great boasting before 1850—was considered a violation of trust. These were the outstanding features of Oxford and Cambridge that produced their claim to be the home of liberal education and

[1] Quoted in Corelli Barnett, *The Collapse of British Power* (London, 1972), 38.
[2] Ibid.

humanistic study; for in other respects they were not far different in kind, although sometimes in quality, from the newer universities. By the end of the nineteenth century, all the English universities mixed vocational, professional, and technological objectives. Classical studies were to be found in London, and a superior school of historical studies at Manchester. In these places the Oxford tone was absent.

If we move away from the social life, from the 'fête champêtre by Watteau',[1] setting to one side those few 'aesthetic dons' who were to exercise a particular influence on certain groups of young men—dons like Pater at Oxford and Lowes Dickinson at Cambridge, exploring ideas of the good and the beautiful, or Jowett and T. H. Green, each with his own views of the connection between learning and life—we pick up another tone. Both professors and tutors had complained repeatedly throughout the century that the scope of their teaching and the amount of freedom they needed to develop their teaching and their scholarship were hampered by the tyranny of examinations, by what the mathematician Augustus De Morgan once called (speaking of the Cambridge tripos) 'the upas tree which poisoned all around it'.[2] The supremacy of the examination system, which had become even more important through its use in the selection of fellows, for appointments to masterships in the leading secondary schools, and as preparation for the higher reaches of the civil service, made innovation in the curriculum difficult. All proposals for change had to be fought out within the faculty boards, in the Senate and in Convocation, making it extremely difficult for individual teachers to modify their teaching, to experiment with new ideas and new methods, or to directly introduce their students to some of the results of the marvellous changes in scholarship and science sweeping across Europe. What was not likely to be tested at the end of three or more years of undergraduate education could not easily be taught, or taught only before small lecture audiences composed of students willing to forego some of the time that might otherwise be used in preparing for the tripos and the schools. The sphinx wanted only certain answers and would devour the passer-by who failed

[1] Ibid, 39.
[2] Alexander Bain, *Dissertations on Leading Philosophical Topics* (London, 1903), 277.

to come up with them. Furthermore, the sphinx could not tell one stranger from another, for all had numbers, not names.

Such a system of education might be called liberal education, although not in Georgian terms, but could the education provided be called humanistic? The syllabus, early specialization, the mind-training, the close association with a rational, bureaucratic State recruiting through examinations, and the anonymity of the entire procedure of testing was not in substance or spirit the education of the whole man. To be sure, the games, the clubs, the debating societies, the plays, the sociability of the collegiate communities were meant to supplement the purely academic education received and to restore the balance. Brought to the universities earlier in the century by undergraduates anxious to vary the boredom of residence and the dreary examination routine in the days when the Oxford syllabus was at its narrowest, games and clubs had come in time to be so much a part of the recreational life of the older universities that they were treated almost as an indispensable part of the teaching. But not quite. Dons were deeply divided over their value, some maintaining that they distracted from learning and the serious purposes of education, that they were philistine and anti-intellectual, encouraged social conformity, and discouraged true independence of self, and others claiming that allowance had to be made for the development of character, for qualities such as loyalty and selflessness, which the training of the mind alone could never do. One group looked outward to the developing world of advancing scholarship, anxious to acquire international reputations for themselves and their institutions. The other group looked inward, desirous of preserving unique traditions and continuity with an aristocratic and privileged past.

It cannot be easily concluded that these two facets of Oxford and Cambridge life in the second half of the nineteenth century comprised a whole view of education. It would be a stretch of the historical imagination to say that Oxford and Cambridge had developed an integrated view of the proper relationship of mind to body. Recreations and examinations were neither integrated nor directed to the requirement of a common national culture. The universities and the colleges within them were insulated and self-contained. Had it been otherwise, there could have been no character formation theory at all in the middle decades of the nineteenth century. As had been so often the case in the history of a liberal education, its several components were separated, and university education was as schizophrenic in Victoria's time as it was in good King George's glorious reign.

12

The Quest for Liberal Education

IT IS possible to speak of the Georgian ideal of a liberal education because the age itself attempted to fashion models and types, being still under the classical influence of archetypes and forms. From the early decades of the nineteenth century the task became more difficult for the same reason: the age was developing a much more plural sense of itself. To be sure, a number of thinkers from one end of the century to the other tried to keep alive the notion of a community of values from which educational ideals would organically derive, and they were not without influence. But the search for a holistic culture remained just that. Indeed, the history of the word 'culture' itself, as its historians have shown, indicates how impossible it was after the French Revolution, the spread of evangelicalism, and the arrival of industrialism to obtain an adequate perspective on the society's moral centre.

1. *Universal Knowledge*

As is so often the case when ideas have lost their traditional context and are in the process of acquiring new meaning, it is easier to decide on what they do not mean than on what they do mean. The writers who discussed liberal education in the middle decades of the nineteenth century were no exception to this rule. They all agreed with the Georgians, for example, that liberal education must not be 'narrow, one-sided and illiberal'. These phrases redound through the nineteenth century, and they certainly are present today. The Victorians also agreed that learning was not to be pedantic and that liberal education had to be more than 'merely' useful. They also—or many of them—concluded

146

that liberal education must always serve some higher purpose and that, consequently, whoever receives a liberal education must be in some way permanently influenced by it. The experience of a liberal education would be wasted, the Victorians believed, unless some unique benefit accrued.

Agreed on these points, they nevertheless divided over how best to achieve them, or even what they meant. What, after all, was a narrow, one-sided, and illiberal education? Was it the study of classical languages, which all mid-Victorians admitted was commonly synonymous with liberal education? The defenders said that certainly classical studies achieved the purposes of liberal education best. The study of classics improved taste by forming it on the highest standards, furthered the art of public speaking, strengthened the reading and writing of English, transmitted correct moral ideas, and, of course, disciplined the cognitive faculties. Another argument, that the study of Latin and Greek was essential to such professions as the Church, Law, and Medicine, only muddied the waters, as liberal education was not supposed to be 'merely' useful—that is, vocational—and it could easily be rejoined that lawyers and physicians could live and practise without Latin and Greek. A wag—and there were some —could even suggest other branches of learning as more appropriate.

Each of the arguments in support of classical education as the supreme means of achieving liberal education could be refuted by employing the traditional criteria that it should not be narrow, one-sided, and consequently illiberal. What, after all, was taste? 'A certain delicate fastidiousness, a finical fine-ladyism of the intellect, which I hold to be essentially pernicious . . . it values manner more than matter.'[1] This was the answer of one Victorian churchman-reformer who laughed at the Georgian practise of falling short of its declared ideals. Taste was civilization *manqué*. And what, in fact, were the best models upon which taste was to be based? A matter to be debated, no doubt, once Taste had vanished.

There was naturally the question of taste for what? If for writing, why read Aristotle, who hardly embodied the perfection of form in his own style? The same could be said for other classical

---

[1] F. W. Farrar, *Essays on a Liberal Education* (London, 1867), 222.

authors. As to the matter of whether the study of classics furthers the art of public speaking—possibly, if the public speaking is done in Latin. Otherwise, each language has its own rules of rhetoric. And is public speaking, in fact, the true end of liberal instruction? There is the problem of learning to express thoughts clearly on paper. Surely Latin and Greek improve the writing of English? Why should they? If each language has its own rules of rhetoric, so has it singular rules of composition, and no single language, as the linguists demonstrated, is 'perfect'. Well, then, classical literature transmits 'correct' moral ideas. Then Aristophanes, Apuleius, Catullus, and Petronius, among others, must be kept out of the hands of young persons. What can we say for the claim that classical languages discipline the cognitive faculties? That this is true and valuable, but could also be accomplished by modern languages; and in disciplining other faculties —for example, observation and reasoning—natural and physical science were doubtless superior. What are we finally to conclude about the teaching of classics as part of a liberal education? That the study of classical languages enslaved the mind to *words* and kept it from learning *things*, that classical languages were taught for grammar and verse composition, but not for the ideas of the authors themselves. Thus cut off from other branches of learning and confined to only portions of the classical heritage, they were taught pedantically. Finally, it had to be said that the study of classical languages was narrow, one-sided, and illiberal.

This was no doubt a satisfying attack on the claims of classical education by those who made it in the middle decades of the nineteenth century. It could conceivably have been made in the eighteenth century, and to a certain extent it was; but the attack failed intellectually to dislodge classical learning because of its total identification with the elite culture of the period, because of its intricate relationship to the values of right living. But in the nineteenth century, without that organic support, virtually the only successful defence that classicists could make, at least on intellectual grounds, was in the value of composition, of construing and parsing as mind discipline, but even for those purposes modern languages could be employed.

The logical conclusion of the debate was that the study of classics was only useful for itself, for the training of teachers of classics. Whereas it might be comforting for opponents to triumph in this way, to do so was shortsighted. For all subjects foundered on the same rock. None could claim to substitute for classics as the principal medium of liberal education, for none could convince all members of the educational establishment that it more than others disciplined all or most faculties. The only answer, then, was for a liberal education to become truly general education, to unite languages and natural or experimental science, or, as one Victorian put it, 'A man of the highest education ought to know something of everything, and everything of something.'[1]

This conclusion was arrived at in the middle decades of the nineteenth century. At first glance, it seems to be related to the amateur model of a man who might be able to dance or play a musical instrument or translate from the classics, but not too well, for that would make him an expert, and the man who was an expert could not be broad or liberal. But actually it bore only the vaguest relationship to the dilettante ideal of the past. To appreciate this, we must look more closely at the characteristic statements of men espousing what was in fact a new position, at least in a long time: the ideal of universal knowledge.

'A liberal education', wrote the gracious scholar and leading utilitarian philosopher, Henry Sidgwick, 'has for its object to impart the highest culture, to lead youths to the most full, vigorous, and harmonious exercise, according to the best ideal attainable, of their active, cognitive, and aesthetic faculties.'[2]

This is a promising and rich statement of the purpose of a liberal education, and it turns about the meaning of a central term, 'culture'. In the use of this word we seem to approach in spirit what the Georgians had aspired to and missed when 'civility' failed to become 'civilization'. The great mid-century definition of culture is naturally Matthew Arnold's, and indeed his use of the word comes closer than any other nineteenth-century formulation to some of the urgent goals of Georgian morality. In fact, Arnold's culture is a brilliant restatement of the central tenets of the eighteenth-century idea of a liberal education. There are many aspects of the inheritance present in his thought, but the three most pertinent—his leading conclusions—should suffice for the moment. The first is the notion of a holistic culture, where self and society are integrated and

[1] Ibid., 258.
[2] Ibid., 87.

in accord, so that education is harmonious with the stated aims of society. The second is intimately related to the first and returns the civilizing ideal to its specific meaning. Culture is a restraining force, an internalized discipline opposing itself to anarchy and requiring the subordination of private inclinations to public welfare. The third conclusion is the idea of a standard based on commonly-accepted canons of taste, summed up in the enchanting refrain, 'the best that has been thought and said.'

This is, however, as close to the eighteenth century as the Victorians came, for Arnold's definition of culture was not accepted by Sidgwick. It was, for him, too nostalgic, too aristocratic, and too much a refutation of individualism. What was needed, said Sidgwick and the other Victorians, was a definition of culture that was pertinent to the problems of an industrial and increasingly democratic society, one that was not *au fond* reactionary. But when asked to produce a definition that would exactly suit the requirements of industrial society, thus stating what he meant by liberal education, Sidgwick hesitated. 'What this ideal, this culture may be,' he pondered, 'is not easy to determine.'[1]

Elsewhere in the same essay, published in the 1860s, the decade in which Arnold's 'culture' was being hotly discussed, Sidgwick approached the meaning of a liberal education from a different direction. 'The summit of a liberal education,' he stated, 'the crown of the highest culture, is Philosophy—meaning by Philosophy the sustained effort, if it be no more than an effort, to frame a complete and reasoned synthesis of the facts of the universe.'[2]

The ideal of universal knowledge which is here referred to is an echo of scholastic methods of synthesis, but it was influenced more by nineteenth-century German neo-idealism and French positivism than by any yearning for medieval models. The search for underlying philosophical principles of organization or the nomothetic arrangement of historical materials or even the employment of theories of biological evolution to arrange factual materials is characteristic of English thinkers in or out of academic life in the decades following 1850. Thus Halford Vaughan argued that while the proximate end of liberal education

[1] Ibid.
[2] Ibid., 140.

was faculty discipline, the final end was the derivation of a system of morality from the collation of widely gathered materials; and the famous Mark Pattison, who became the Rector of Lincoln College, Oxford, after a life of many disappointments, believed that liberal education ought to approximate 'the speculative vigour of the middle age University'.[1] Writing in the period of renewed interest in the possibilities of character formation to solve some of the teaching problems of Oxford colleges, he also found a place in Oxford studies for some of the older objectives of liberal education, for 'the humane polish and elegant studies of the classical revival'. The two, he thought, would form an excellent association. But he revealed the primary direction of his thinking when he criticized French liberal education for its lack of philosophical seriousness and for its frivolous view of the usefulness of education. 'Liberal education in France is not yet considered worth having for its own sake, or as a qualification for *life*; it is wholly subordinate to the purpose of shining in society; only so much of it is attained as shall serve as a qualification for *conversation*.'[2] Clearly, if liberal education was to have some connection with life—here vaguely expressed—it was not meant to have merely a polite function. Education for the purpose of social intercourse—an appropriate end of education for a Georgian moralist like Jane Austen—he considered superficial and vain.

The new ideal of universal knowledge can be regarded as a repudiation of the course of liberal education as it developed following the close of the Georgian era. It can be viewed as a protest against the fragmentation of learning and the narrow specialism that resulted from the hegemony of the examination system, and many leading Victorian thinkers did, in fact, so view it. As such, it seems to point backwards towards the eighteenth century, to a time when classical learning at least seemed to form an integrated body of knowledge animated by a philosophical conception of the value of literature to life and not solely by a gymnastic psychological theory. But however backward certain aspects of the ideal of universal knowledge might appear, the conception was firmly rooted in the nineteenth century. The

[1] Mark Pattison, *Essays*, collected and arranged by Henry Nettleship, I (Oxford, 1889), 482.
[2] Ibid.

emphasis in the theory of universal knowledge was passive, not active. The higher culture, the higher morality, the 'higher liberal education'—we encounter this phrase for the first time in the mid nineteenth century—were achievements of the contemplative mind. This was a scholar's or a scribe's or a sage's formulation, an opting for Martha rather than Mary. It was not at all addressed to the question of the whole man. And while it may have subordinated the training of the mind to the question of the ultimate use of mind, it obviously justified on new grounds cerebral educational doctrines like those of faculty psychology.

The conception of universal knowledge answered the criteria of a liberal education that it must not be narrow, one-sided, and illiberal. The comprehensive survey of all knowledge and the synthetic integration of information collected from all branches of learning were guarantees that liberal education would not be pedantic and that it would be broad. It also guaranteed that it would not be 'merely' useful, for universal knowledge was no more vocational than the study of classical grammar and syntax. But while apparent that universal knowledge was not merely useful, the question was bound to arise whether it was useful at all. Had not Sidgwick himself argued that one of the great defects of classical education was that it was 'artificial'—i.e., that it bore little or no relation to what its recipient might do in later life? Science, he thought, was 'natural' or useful precisely because it did have a direct impact on the quality of material life.

The question of usefulness or utility had always been the central difficulty of any attempt to define a liberal education because it established the point at which liberal separated from illiberal education, where the freeman could be distinguished from the slave and the liberal mind from the servile one. But from its earliest appearance in the Georgian period, the question of usefulness was perplexing. The Georgian definition of utility had depended upon a status difference, on the distance between certain occupations and others. Therefore, the definition began, or was predicated upon, existing discrepancies in position, rank, and wealth. It was assumed that only the highest ranks of society needed education for style. But this assumption had unexpected consequences. The eighteenth century rediscovered the true flexibility of the cortegiano ideal: that in the right historical circumstances style made the man—any man (and the woman, too—

witness the extraordinary proliferation of boarding schools for girls of nearly all classes in the late eighteenth century). A liberal education, especially for members of newly emerging service occupations, could be used to conceal original status differences. Hence there was wide support for the notion that education should inculcate manners, that liberal education must be social not vocational. Furthermore, since for so many important members of English society getting-along was the best means of getting-on, knowledge or skills of any kind had to be subordinate. Since sociability was the channel to careers, it was unnecessary to focus on job preparation in education. One anonymous Georgian writer of 1734 even implied that education called 'liberal' was only so by default, that if jobs were more certain—he was, of course, thinking only of certain kinds of employment—it would be advantageous to prepare more directly. Beginning his discussion with the lofty Georgian dictum that 'the Business of Education is to disengage a Man from all Prejudices,'[1] he argued at the very same time that the difficulty of finding friends in the right places was the real reason for general education. Uncertainty of employment, he said, makes it necessary for the student 'to enter into parts of Learning, which perhaps will be but of little use to him in his future way of life, but which, had he gone into some other Path, would have been absolutely necessary.'[2] Flexibility and breadth in education, he is actually saying, have nothing to do with ideals or morality, but are functions of the market. Liberal education is only possible when a man does not know what position he will occupy in life.

In the nineteenth century social class or status differences did not disappear from considerations of education, as the famous three-levels of education statement in the 1860s report of the Taunton Commission on secondary education indicates, but in general it was assumed that some degree of social mobility would prevail, and that ultimately freedom of economic opportunity would be the rule. The spread of examinations throughout the society supported—in principle, at least—the theory of advancement through achievement. That principle, as we know, was much compromised in practice, owing to the absence of a satisfactory state-supported elementary and secondary system of

[1] *Of Education* (London, 1734), 17. British Museum 1031.g.7 (10).
[2] Ibid.

national education, to social and economic disadvantages in upbringing, and to the survival of a network of special interests. But most writers in the second half of the nineteenth century assumed that the future elite would be increasingly recruited on democratic grounds and devised their theories on this premise.

The question they posed for themselves was what kind of education was suitable for a meritocratic society, for an industrial society, and for an increasingly democratic society, or, rather, what kind of education was suitable for the leaders of such a society, for they regarded differential standards of education and variations of education according to intended vocation as unavoidable. For one group of writers, the ideal of universal knowledge was the appropriate answer, for it was, they argued, pre-eminently useful and not 'merely' useful. The challenge of industrial society was the foremost challenge education had ever faced, and therefore only the highest form of education could meet it. Industrial society was new, it overturned all known values and institutions, it moved at a speed unprecedented in history, and it brought more actors on to the historical stage than had ever before been accommodated. Living in such a society— always restless and impatient, always demanding and unstable, without a centre and without a common core of values— required more than style, conversation, or manners; more than sociability, liberality, and civility. It required leaders who grasped the magnitude of the problems before them and by an effort of speculative imagination, based on a solid understanding of the meaning of industrialism in the context of world history, would be able to give the turbulent society a proper sense of its character and its mission, directing it towards the realization of its uncommon potential. Universal knowledge alone could accomplish this. It was a magnificent effort of the rational mind. It would grasp and control the direction of change and, by so doing, give comfort and assurance to a civilization in the first struggles of birth.

This summary of the uses to which universal knowledge was to be put conveys more confidence in the ideal than was actually held by those who professed it. The monumentality of the self-imposed task was overwhelming, and few mid-Victorian thinkers possessed the requisite assurance needed to cope with the problems of industrial change. For despite the breathtaking dimensions of their rhetoric, intended to be on the same scale of magnitude as the breathtaking forces transforming Victorian society, their answers ultimately fell back to a different level of justification for liberal education. We do not know, they confessed, what form of morality, what kind of culture, or exactly what sort of qualities are needed to direct an industrial society. We only know that intellect must make an effort to find out, that it must penetrate to the heart of the new society, discover the facts of its existence, and organize those facts into a coherent whole, from which, some day, hopefully, an answer will emerge enabling us to cope with the phenomenon of change. But even this overstates the confidence of their views. Finally, for them a liberal education was a celebration of intellect itself, the *telos* of evolution; and perhaps all the reasoning mind could do was sit back and 'examine, comprehensively and closely, the wonderful scale of methods by which the human mind has achieved its various degrees of conquest over the world of sense.'[1]

The foregoing illustrations of the use of a liberal education are drawn from the writings of Oxbridge men who were directly involved in the mid-century battles over the reorganization of both collegiate and professorial teaching. They were men who had themselves been undergraduates at the two senior universities of England, had grown up there in the days of the clerical supremacy—indeed, one of them, Pattison, was in holy orders—and had been exposed both at school and university to a classical education. They were freely conversant with the peculiarities and intricacies of Oxford and Cambridge politics; their views were shaped in communities isolated from the industrial centres of England.

A very different personality of even greater reputation was the physician and scientist, Thomas Henry Huxley. His education took place in the new university colleges of London, and he passed his life in medical schools and technical colleges. He had close ties to the Nonconformist communities of industrial England, encouraged the foundation and spread of the new civic universities, and promoted the extension of scientific knowledge and learning. He was also, however, like Vaughan, Sidgwick, Pattison, or Sir Robert Seeley, interested in synthetic

[1] Farrar, 140.

learning and the unity of knowledge. He, too, expressed himself on the meaning and uses of a liberal education. In a speech to the South London Working Men's College in 1868 (the composition of the audience is itself a striking indication of change), he developed the following interpretation of the character of a general education: 'That man ... has had a liberal education, who has been so trained in youth that his body is the ready servant of his will, and does with ease and pleasure all the work that, as a mechanism, it is capable of; whose intellect is a clear, cold, logic engine, with all its parts of equal strength, and in smooth working order; ready, like a steam engine, to be turned to any kind of work, and spin the gossamers as well as forge the anchors of the mind; whose mind is stored with a knowledge of the great and fundamental truths of Nature and of the laws of her operations; one who, no stunted ascetic, is full of life and fire, but whose passions are trained to come to heel by a vigorous will, the servant of a tender conscience; who has learned to love all beauty, whether in Nature or of art, to hate all vileness, and to respect others such as himself.

'Such an one and no other, I conceive, has had a liberal education; for he is, as completely as a man can be, in harmony with Nature.'[1]

This is a remarkable portrait of an educated man. The mind is a steam engine, cold one minute and hot the next, so that the swift change in temperature can operate the mechanism and release the awesome power. The contrasting images continue throughout the definition. The passions are cooled—held in check by a 'vigorous will'; but the personality is also 'full of life and fire'. The mind is sometimes cool or still—it forges anchors; but it is sometimes hot and in movement—it spins gossamers. The central feature of the portrait is the tension between opposites, not a balance of qualities, and the purpose of a liberal education is not the calm contemplation of the achievements of intellect over the centuries, but the need to move mountains, confidently, steadily.

In this definition, we also encounter a number of familiar phrases and ideas. The mind 'stored with a knowledge of the great and fundamental truths of Nature' and 'in harmony with

[1] Thomas Henry Huxley, 'A Liberal Education: And Where to Find It', in *Lay Sermons, Addresses, and Reviews* (London, 1870), 39–40.

Nature' could have been spoken at any time in the eighteenth century. The man who has learned to control himself, to hate ugliness and love beauty, is a Georgian type, and the attack on the ascetic is also Georgian, the dislike of withdrawal. The mind as a steam engine able to accomplish any task set before it has an echo, although a strange one, of the ideal of breadth present in the older concept of a liberal education. But despite these survivals the differences are fundamental. There is nothing 'polite' about the mind spinning gossamers or forging anchors, and while there is a certain humanity in the definition—the man of tender conscience who respects others as himself—this is far from Georgian sociability. The entire tone and feeling of the passage and the images employed come straight from an industrial society. Whatever is left of the Georgian ideal of a liberal education in Huxley's rendering of it does not easily combine with the later additions. It is not so much that the symmetry of the older view is severely disturbed as that the threads piece together to form entirely new cloth. Here again, as with so many other features of liberal education in the nineteenth century, the discontinuities are more compelling than the continuities.

2. *Idola Novitatis*

Universal knowledge as liberal education bears a relationship to, but is not coterminous with, another educational change that had a more lasting impact on general education, as well as on the structure of higher education and the organization of professional academic life. The change was by no means exclusively English. In fact, once again in the history of education the principal influences crossed the Channel from the Continent. The change was one in attitude towards the importance of accumulating knowledge, and it goes under various names. It is sometimes called, and was called in its time, the search for new knowledge. We know it, and the later nineteenth century was to know it, as the research ideal. And, in general, it is associated with German *Lehrnfreiheit*. In time, the ideal of new knowledge produced the intellectual characteristics now associated with academic work generally: the bold, inquisitive, speculative mind, challenging traditional beliefs and valuing most originality and discovery.

The traditional view of knowledge inherited from the eighteenth century was that by and large a liberal education should be primarily concerned with past learning, with preserving the record of great achievements, and with handing on to succeeding generations the wisdom and benefits of received knowledge. This view of the place of knowledge in liberal education was unquestionably influenced by yet another classical doctrine, very likely Plato's, that art was a copy of *perceptible* nature, while knowledge or philosophy was the contemplation of nature *itself*. The platonic distinction between art and knowledge was actually intended to prove that art was further from reality than knowledge, being a copy of what the eye could see, whereas philosophy was a copy of the ideal forms contemplated by the mind. In the centuries following the Renaissance, it was not appreciated that in the doctrine nature itself was twice removed from reality, and it was assumed that all artists copied reality. And since all artists were inspired by the same platonic aspiration, there could be no objection to selective borrowing from one another. The aesthetic or literary bias of liberal education in the eighteenth century naturally inclined the Georgians to the position that whatever learning a gentleman required could be obtained from traditional models.

Outside the universities *Ars simia naturae* (art the ape of nature) did not go unchallenged by European artists and writers. Both Chardin and Hogarth painted satires of the famous formula. In the later eighteenth century, authors, poets, and artists questioned the significance of copying and debated the value of innovation, or what was called 'invention'. The debate took place all over Europe. Goethe on his Italian journey found it raging in Vicenza in 1786. Reynolds defended the traditional classical concept of copying, so vital to his neoclassical programme, and Blake, who hated that programme, attacked him for it, pronouncing on behalf of the autonomy of the artist. Perhaps he used, as Wittkower has suggested, a theory of genius developed from Aristotle's doctrine of the Saturnine temperament, or from Plato's theory of the *furores*.[1] Chinnery at Oxford gives us a very clear picture of how undergraduates of his day

[1] R. Wittkower, 'Imitation, Eclecticism and Genius', in *Aspects of the Eighteenth Century*, ed. Earl R. Wasserman (Baltimore, 1965); Werner Jaeger, *Aristotle* (London, 1962), 92.

understood and discussed the matter of originality. In a letter to his sister in 1811, he addressed himself to the Reynolds-Blake dispute. Must genius, he asked, be 'bound by the shackles of reason & rule?' He answered his own rhetorical question by taking the safer of the two sides. 'I do not clearly understand why the wild energetic effusions of a creative mind should always and inevitably lose by being brought under some kind of methodical arrangement, or by undergoing some lustral process, which may clear them from the films of their native rudeness, and thus by polishing them render their intrinsic worth more conspicuous to immediate observation.' He warmed to the conclusion: 'I most unequivocally deny that the establishment of methodical rules & the prevalence of criticism have prevented extraordinary works in metaphysics & in the sciences from appearing; for it is the establishment of these very rules which can alone point the way to deeper investigation;—it is the prevalence of this very criticism which can alone be productive of greater & more *accurate* knowledge.'[1]

Three years earlier, in one of his written college themes, Chinnery had discussed the matter from another but parallel perspective by asking himself whether novelty had any value in knowledge or whether novel ideas could make any significant contribution to social and ethical life. Novelty, he wrote, is not the same thing as true greatness, for true greatness grows in our estimation the more we contemplate it, but novelty 'lessens in proportion as we become familiar with the object, and often entirely ceases upon a more intimate acquaintance with it.' Elsewhere in the theme, he admitted that novelty gave rise to excitement and beauty, but he kept his enthusiasm for it in check. Novelty has great destructive power, for it is one of the passions, and therefore must be properly controlled. 'In morals, politics, & government, its innovations are carefully to be guarded against.' Finally, still caught between wanting to say something positive about novelty, but restrained by conventional teachings against it, he concluded that novelty may be all right as a stimulus to fresh inquiry but never for its own sake.[2]

The belief that all wisdom is received and that innovation is

---

[1] Chinnery Papers, 1 February 1811.
[2] Ibid., following letter of 21 October 1808.

primarily a restatement of what is already known dominated the Georgian conception of liberal education. But, as Chinnery indicated in his Christ Church themes, the problem was much greater than the significance of rules in artistic creation. Too much freedom of thought and an unchecked exercise of the imagination were potentially damaging to the existing structure of morals and politics. In the half century after 1770, the authority of a hierarchical society and an Established Church was repeatedly questioned, and university officials worried about the effects of open-ended inquiry on the undergraduates placed in their charge. To expose young persons to an educational ideal that emphasized new knowledge was to admit to uncertainties in received knowledge. It might lead to heresy, it could be socially disruptive, and certainly, given Georgian assumptions about individual autonomy, psychically damaging.

Accordingly, while undergraduates discussed the delights and dangers of innovative thought, dons were taking a conservative position and were attempting to put the damper on wide-ranging exploration of the implications of novelty, originality, and invention. They insisted that it was more important for a university and for liberal education to preserve the received body of learning and to pass it on than to encourage the search for fresh knowledge.

Consequently, we hear repeated over and over again the undesirability of allowing too much scope for intellectual independence in serious questions of Church and State. In a sermon preached at Cambridge in 1795, it was said 'that a system of education which has for its chief object the cultivation and improvement of the reasoning Powers, is liable, like all other things, to perversion and abuse.'[1] The famous Scottish scientist, Brewster, distinguished between the botanist, his eyes fixed on the earth, and the astronomer, his mind lost in the stars. Speculation, he cautioned, engendered doubt, and doubt was the parent either of apathy or impiety.[2] Defending the Oxford curriculum of

[1] John Mainwaring, *A Sermon Preached before the University of Cambridge on the Third of May, 1795* (Cambridge, 1795), 14.

[2] This point is elaborated philosophically by Edgar Morse, 'Natural Philosophy, Hypothesis, and Impiety: Sir David Brewster Confronts the Undulatory Theory of Light' (unpublished doctoral dissertation, University of California, Berkeley, 1972).

1810, a lay supporter argued that knowledge might bedazzle and
confuse young men and encourage their vanity.[1] 'To *aim* at
novelty,' wrote Edward Hawkins on becoming the first Dean
Ireland's Professor at Oxford in 1848, 'is even one of the prime
temptations of a Teacher, but it is little less than the abuse of his
office.'[2] In the same way, Pusey, leading the high church party at
Oxford, opposed in 1852 the new tendency for professors to copy
the German role model. 'They form to themselves the ideal of
some Professor as . . . Niebuhr, or De Sacy, or Bopp, or Gesenius,
persons who advance the general knowledge of the subject, or, in
secular matters, strike out new lines of thought.'[3] It must be said,
however, that in Pusey's time the new tendency that he deplored
was already so prevalent that he himself in his theological lectures
employed German thought, learning, and sources. 'Of all the
Professors in Oxford,' wrote Dean Stanley, who was astounded
by what he heard in Pusey's lectures, 'there is none who has more
frequently recurred to me as the example of what a German Professor is, and of what an English Professor might be than the
present Regius Professor of Hebrew.'[4]

The famous Cambridge professors of the 1830s and 1840s,
Adam Sedgwick and William Whewell, who wrote books on the
meaning and definition of a liberal education and brought to
their discussions of education the prestige of their accomplishments in science and scholarship, did not believe that anything
fundamentally new would result from research. 'The old truths
will always be true, and always essential,' wrote Whewell. He
was not opposed to the search for new knowledge, but he did
not believe it had any place in undergraduate teaching, where
the 'sound and liberal cultivation of the faculties' was the first
object. The mature man who left the university after acquiring
a thorough appreciation of 'undoubted truths' and 'works of
unquestioned excellence' could safely be allowed a critical
review of the doctrines presented to him. But younger men were
not ready to exercise their own judgement in such matters, and,

[1] Henry Home Drummond, *Observations Suggested by the Strictures of
the Edinburgh Review* (Edinburgh, 1810).
[2] Edward Hawkins, *An Inaugural Lecture* (London, 1848), 27.
[3] Report of the Oxford University Commissioners, Parliamentary
Papers 1852, LVII. Evidence, 14.
[4] Bill, 253.

if allowed the privilege of speculation, would put in 'serious and extensive jeopardy the interests of the civilization of England and the world'.[1]

Whewell believed in a world of final causes, where fresh knowledge corroborated old knowledge, deepening the observer's understanding of known effects and causes. The religious revivals, high and low, at Oxford and Cambridge in the early Victorian period restored a religious perspective to the place of knowledge in the university to many of the most serious minds in higher education. The next generation was to react strongly to evangelicalism and ritualism and return learning to the secularism it had acquired in the eighteenth century. But for Whewell and minds like Newman's there were limits to what intellect without grace or revelation could achieve and barriers beyond which discovery could not advance. Especially was education alone powerless to elucidate man's perception of his moral role. Whewell's Cambridge colleague, Adam Sedgwick, shared his belief in a world of final causes. For him, too, knowledge and teaching were intended to explain the order of the universe that was God's making; and the role of the university and aim of a liberal education were to teach that order to undergraduates so that they could tell right from wrong. There was still something Georgian in this, no doubt. Sedgwick even wrote that in classical literature 'We seek for examples and maxims of prudence and models of taste.'[2] But there was a difference. A Georgian would consider the violation of examples and maxims of prudence a breach of taste; but for Sedgwick it was a moral infraction.

'Pedantry' the Georgians had called the search for new knowledge. The desire for novelty was dangerous to teaching. There is a theme here that has not altogether disappeared from the meaning of a liberal education, but it is presently a minor theme. *Idola novitatis*, the art historian Gombrich has recently called the modern university search for originality. 'The humanist remains to some extent a guardian of texts, novelty is not his

[1] Quoted in Robert G. McPherson, *The Theory of Higher Education in Nineteenth-Century England* (Athens, Georgia, 1959), 49–51.

[2] Adam Sedgwick, *A Discourse on the Studies of the University*, eds. Eric Ashby and Mary Anderson (Leicester, 1969), 9.

prime concern.'[1] The eighteenth-century Enlightenment mind prided itself on being free of error and delusion, liberated from the folly of superstition, and completely responsive to reason. And well might it so pride itself. But we must always remember the circles of restraints within which Georgian intellectual speculation operated and the cultural limits of many of its leading conceptions. The eighteenth-century mind that was to be free of error and delusion nevertheless still operated in a teleological world where innovation itself was relatively unimportant. It was not a world in which the exercise of the critical intelligence for its own sake was a cardinal value. To be sure, the word 'critic' was significant in the period, being associated with the rise in status and importance of the Georgian writer and intellectual, Scottish as well as English. But to be a critic meant to be able to discern and judge according to universal or general principles of taste or according to rules: in poetry, in art, in the theatre, in life.

These were not supposed to be arbitrary principles, nor were they to be derived from personal experience. They were to be 'scientifick', the word Johnson uses in one of those few places where he defends Addison against the opinion that his criticism was not based on principles of human nature. For the Scots criticism meant establishing standards of civilized behaviour and indeed civilization through a systematic inquiry into the human condition. Above all, civilization meant restraining the passions and exercising self-discipline and not yielding to wild and savage impulses or unchecked fantasies of the imagination. Yet even criticism had its dangers. It was commonly recognized that even in the Georgian use of the word 'critic' there were implicit threats to the meaning of liberal education. Joseph Wharton, who put literary criticism on a new historical footing in the second half of the eighteenth century, and Oliver Goldsmith, whose name is more familiar to the general reader today, both understood that criticism destroyed polite learning.[2] Hence criticism was not allowed to become a fully open-ended activity. It was hedged in, constrained by the idea of a standard Taste.

---

[1] E. H. Gombrich, 'Research in the Humanities: Ideals and Idols', in *Daedalus* (Spring, 1973), 5.

[2] Pittock, 84, 148.

Although in England that idea was nearly stretched out of shape in its own lifetime, the universities clung to it.

3. *New Knowledge*

There can be no doubt that in certain respects Whewell, Sedgwick, Pusey, Newman, and all their Georgian predecessors who worried about the implications of novelty were right in thinking that the principle of art aping nature had proven itself over the centuries. It created a vast community of common discourse among educated men and provided them with the shared familiarity of a select, but not confined, range of materials. The devotion paid to past models produced a stunning and creative adaptation of inherited forms, motifs, themes, styles, and subjects that unequivocally merit the compliment (from our point of view) 'original'. But, true as this is, it is still necessary to distinguish between originality which is imitative in character, taking as its point of departure an admired authority, and creative work which is no longer conscious of models of excellence and claims, rightly or wrongly, to be venturing upon totally uncharted waters. Belief in a world where innovation does not have a primary role, where new learning is not recognized as such but is instantly made into a confirmation of what is already known, does prevent the complicated process of creativity from having an ideological component. Discovery is not considered a conscious and primary objective. The ramifications of an innovation may not be apparent, or the implications of a discovery may be resisted. There is no intellectual imperative, so to speak, continually directing the active intelligence towards the goal of novelty, thus influencing the pace of discovery and its nature, the value accorded to it, and the development of standards to measure it. No special encouragement is given to the pursuit of discovery, and no reward allowed for it.

These are the considerations that must inevitably set off the last decades of the nineteenth century from most of what went before in determining the overall meaning of a liberal education. They justify use of the phrase 'knowledge revolution' to describe the transformation that occurred within the universities of Europe when they dropped the museum concept of a university —a place to store and admire the marvellous achievements of the past—and adopted a dynamic and open-ended conception of knowledge.

The knowledge revolution is so profound a change that it is difficult to explain how precisely it could have happened. Like all revolutions in culture, it did not occur overnight, nor did it occur simply because there were developments in other countries to be used as examples. For German intellectual achievement to be appreciated in Britain, there had to be, to begin with, a predisposition to accept the fundamental assumptions behind the idea of new knowledge. Simple contact and exposure are not sufficient; for these, as is well known, are frequently double-edged. They enforce national prejudice and insularity as much as they challenge them. Dr. Johnson's response to the excitement of travel and to the alleged benefits of new experience was to deny them any importance whatsoever. There was little to be learned from direct contact, for, as he put it, a blade of grass in France was the same as one in England.

The knowledge revolution was so much an expression of the total transformations in English social and economic life in the nineteenth century that no single factor can be called decisive. No doubt the romantic interest in the exotic and unusual prepared the way, as did the increasing contact between the English and non-Europeans of different culture, heritage, values, and language, as in the Indian subcontinent. Possibly the reviving interest in medical education that sent Englishmen and Scots to Paris in the 1840s produced a greater awareness of the deficiencies in higher education at home and stimulated a desire for reform. Very likely, too, a developing role crisis occurring within the academic communities of Oxford and Cambridge in the 1850s publicized the achievements of German scholarship and science and led to widespread dissatisfaction with the education provided in the leading institutions of England. The structure of teaching and scholarship at Oxford and Cambridge had long been unstable. The purpose of the fellowship system was to spread the wealth among young men who had distinguished themselves in the examinations, but not to build up a permanent academic staff. The professoriate, with the exception of holders of divinity chairs, was inadequately paid, and the professorial role, like that of the college fellow, was ancillary to the examination system. In addition, most of the new subjects being de-

veloped in the German universities and even scientific subjects
well advanced in England were hardly provided for. The university system was capable of producing a certain level of
efficient teaching, although scarcely distinguishable from the
best teaching students experienced in their secondary schools,
but it was not capable of guaranteeing viable careers to promising
young men who might be interested in becoming practising
scholars and scientists.

Once generated, the interest in new knowledge advanced very
rapidly as England became locked into industrial and commercial rivalry with France and Germany and later with the
United States. Modifications in the structure of industry and
changes in product demanded more systematic scientific and
engineering training, as well as a need for better educated
managerial staff. In the 1860s, 1870s, and 1880s English industry
was heavily reliant on German and Swiss talents in all levels of
enterprise. In government the remarkable growth of social
administration, the establishment gradually of national systems
of primary and secondary education, and simply the burden of
preparing government business produced the need for a professional, if not exactly an expert, bureaucracy and encouraged
the development of all branches of academic study. In fact, it
was government pressure rather than business pressure that
really stirred the late nineteenth-century interest in science,
applied science, and technology, and it was government fears
about the problem of imperial supremacy that pushed the
universities towards the production of new knowledge. Additional pressure came from changes in the structure of professional
life and from the growth of new professions, dependent by
definition on higher education.

The greatest Continental influence on England, both quanti-
tatively and qualitatively, was, of course, German. Englishmen
had been going to Germany as students rather than as tourists
since the end of the 1820s, and the numbers were much greater
after the 1840s. J. M. Kemble, who had not distinguished himself at Cambridge in the official studies of the university, travelled
to Munich in 1829 to read Kant, went on to Berlin to study
Teutonic philology under Jakob Grimm, and returned to
England in 1832. He is credited with having made critical contributions to the study of Anglo-Saxon. Examples of Englishmen

benefiting from exposure to the lectures of German professors can be cited from all fields except physics and mathematics, where English achievements continued to be brilliant and the admiration of Europe. The great German university chemical laboratories attracted some of the most famous scientific minds of Victorian England. Liebig's laboratory at Giessen and Bunsen's at Heidelberg were renowned in the mid-Victorian period, and a little later in the 1870s Englishmen were attracted to Wundt's famous physiological laboratory in Leipzig, where particularly that interesting mind and peculiar personality, James Ward, went to study. Before Leipzig, he had been at Berlin to listen to Dorner discuss theology and at Goettingen to hear Lotze. German speculation and intellectual advances transformed the importance and meaning of knowledge in science, technology, and—easily as important as the other two for the history of liberal education—*Geisteswissenschaften*, the 'humanistic sciences': Biblical criticism and theology, mythology, ethnology, comparative historical philology, all fields of history, archaeology, literature, and language. German theories of the evolutionary differentiation of all social and political institutions from common simple beginnings gave the enormous quantity of new information a centre and a reason. German emigrés from the revolution of 1848 contributed heavily to the spread of German ideas in England by translating books and by teaching the language to encourage reading in the original.

The research ideal spread with extraordinary rapidity through all levels of education and altered completely the contexts in which all ideas of liberal education were held. Every existing theory of liberal education was revised to accommodate it. Proponents of character formation, who still clung to the belief that the direct purpose of education was preparation for a particular form of social conduct, had to acknowledge that the complexity of living in a technological society demanded some deeper grasp of fact and theory. Supporters of various versions of Arnoldian culture, who were in major respects close to the adherents of character formation, also had to reconsider some of their leading assumptions. The reading of selected great authors to discover a common core of values appeared to be a superficial procedure for understanding self and society when international scholarship in the humanistic sciences was uncovering a remarkable range of information about social existence. And even the supporters of universal knowledge, who were closest to appreciating the ideal of advancing knowledge, were overwhelmed by the cumulative mass of information generated by an academic community expanding rapidly in numbers and output. The integration of the many fields of science and scholarship could not keep pace with the results of compartmentalized research.

The research ideal, therefore, forced adherents of the various kinds of liberal education to question the assumptions and purposes of their theories. But there was, at the same time, another and more positive effect. The research ideal gave new life to the subjects of which all liberal education theories were composed. Operating with the force of an ideology, the ideal of new knowledge eventually pushed all branches of learning to new levels of achievement. The history of classical learning, the traditional backbone of liberal education, and developments in the field of literature generally, the branch of knowledge to which the Georgian theory of liberal education was particularly attached, show this very clearly. They also illustrate how the higher learning and higher critical scholarship decisively broke a deeply rooted understanding of the connection between education and everyday life.

We will recall that the teaching of classics was one of the main targets of the supporters of universal knowledge. It was argued that a comprehensive theory of knowledge was needed precisely because classical education failed to achieve the required dimensions of liberal education. Despite all the archaeological excavations in southern Italy, the new work that had been done in Greek philosophy and in classical philology, the teaching of classics remained essentially the routine of grammar and composition. While, of course, the classical curriculum was certainly broader than this, the attention devoted to the actual content and meaning of the texts being read was secondary. Furthermore, even for the scholars themselves the principal use of classical languages was what it had been for centuries—textual emendation. The advocates of universal knowledge deplored this specialism, although, at the same time, they admitted its uses as mental discipline. Their overall objective, however, was to decrease the amount of time given to classical languages in the liberal arts curriculum, and to vary the overall programme of studies. At the same time, they gave coherence to that programme by holding out the promise of a union of all branches of knowledge.

It is one of the ironies of the history of a liberal education in England that although the intention of the proponents of universal knowledge was to diminish the place of classical education in liberal education, they failed to do so precisely because of the rise of the research ideal. Instead of being demoted by the ethic of new knowledge, classical learning at the universities took advantage of its enormous existing base of financial support and flourished. Furthermore, classical teaching continued to occupy an important place in the curriculum of the principal feeder schools because the nineteenth-century university had once again assumed educational leadership. The examination system joined school to university in a tighter relationship than they had ever had in the Georgian period. What was set in the scholarship examinations devised by the universities was taught in the sixth forms of public and grammar schools.

Classical scholars were among the most prominent academicians of the last quarter of the nineteenth century in proclaiming the advantages of the research ideal, and classical scholars are among the greatest names in university history in the late Victorian and Edwardian periods, especially Oxbridge history. Nor was it mainly the linguists who were represented. Historians of Greece, professors of philosophy and archaeology, comparative mythologists and anthropologists all extended the dimensions of classical scholarship and contributed to its distinction.

In 1876 the great Oxford classical philologist, Henry Nettleship, who contributed to the famous publicistic work called *Essays on the Endowment of Research*, defined liberal education in this way: it was 'the essence of a liberal education that it should stand in constant relation to the advance of knowledge. Research and discovery are the processes by which truth is directly acquired; education is the preparation of the mind for its reception, and the creation of a truth-loving habit.' Believing that this ideal was absent from Oxford but approached at Cambridge, where the philological emphasis was more important than the philosophical, he publicized scientific methods of language study as examples of 'the higher scholarship', and he advocated instruction by professors—'the natural representatives of learning'. Many years later, he elaborated his view on the importance of scientific methods of research, explaining why it was that only knowledge could ever lead the individual or society to what had always been a goal of liberal education, right conduct, or morality. Only knowledge led to truth, and only truth led to morality. This simply-expressed sequence of a complicated set of ideas also contained a hidden adversary; for in maintaining that research could ultimately lead to the establishment of new foundations for moral behaviour, Nettleship was at the same time arguing that literature was helpless to achieve this cherished purpose. Furthermore, literature was not even knowledge. Its study was 'good and ennobling, as drawing the mind upwards and bracing it to the consideration of sublimity and beauty, [but] it cannot be said to have an actively moral effect.'[1] Insofar as some form of moral behaviour is being identified as the ultimate end of education, we have still another echo of the eighteenth century. But the Georgians would have regarded the means advocated by Nettleship as subversive of the ends. Furthermore, literature or art is deprived of its central role in education.

The refusal to assign an active moral function to what had for so long been regarded as the great purpose of liberal education constitutes yet another decisive break with past tradition. Literature, in the corrupted mimetic doctrine, was a substitute for life, and literature, which, of course, meant classical literature, was liberal precisely because it alone could furnish examples of correct behaviour. The Roman rhetoricians had been read expressly for this purpose, although also for their ornamental qualities. Yet Nettleship refused to allow literature perhaps its oldest educational function, and he separated literature from truth, a decision from which it has never quite recovered.

Nettleship's ejection of literature from the centre of a liberal education was gentle compared to what happened in the closing decades of the nineteenth century. The research ideal was not only used to bludgeon classical literature, it was also used to attack the teaching of all literature not conceived as pure philology or science or as evidence for historical development. The result was to delay the establishment of literature as a major university subject until well into the twentieth century, unless literature

[1] Henry Nettleship, *Lectures and Essays*, ed. Francis John Haverfield (Oxford, 1895), 173, 179, 195, 196.

was taught as an adjunct to the historical and linguistic sciences. Literature taught as a source of values or as a response of the emotional life to conditions of human existence was considered merely 'literary criticism' in the decades before the first world war, and as such was completely suspect. The study of literature as literature suffered from its historical association with theories of character formation. As late as 1891, there was no chair in English literary criticism in Oxford among the eighteen chairs and readerships in languages. What was studied were the structures and principles of language, classical languages, of course, or Middle English, Sanskrit, and exotic or forgotten languages. An attempt to establish a school of English studies that would emphasize, among other things, the content of modern literature failed in the 1880s, and the controversy spilled over into the pages of *The Times*. One of the principal participants, the historian E. A. Freeman, whose election to the Regius Professorship of Modern History in 1884 depressed Matthew Arnold, argued that literary criticism could not be the basis for a school of English studies because it was unsuited for examination purposes. Universities could not examine in 'literary criticism', for only 'technical and positive information' could be tested. Literary criticism amounted to no more than personal tastes and preferences. It lacked truth or a factual base, it possessed no scientific methods of analysis and no scientific standing. There was no standard of accuracy against which the conclusions of literary critics could be measured, and therefore literary criticism did not deserve a place in liberal education.[1]

Possibly the greatest attack on the entire mimetic tradition of literature substituting for life, to include the Arnoldian restatement of it, came in an uncompromising Cambridge inaugural lecture delivered on 9 May 1911 by the poet and Latinist, A. E. Housman. The lecture was printed for the first time only a few years ago. In it Housman declared the total divorce of ancient literature taught at the university from literature in general. Classical literature was nothing less than a department of science. 'Scholarship, in short, is not literary criticism.' Housman went on to thoroughly demolish the equation of art with morality,

---

[1] John Churton Collins, *The Study of English Literature* (London, 1891), 12, 12n, 27, 40, 41. See also D. J. Palmer, *The Rise of English Studies* (London, 1965).

much as Nettleship had earlier done, but in his attack art became a threat to the higher values of civilization (a position not so preposterous if we recall Marinetti's *Futurist Manifesto*, published in the same year as Housman's inaugural lecture): 'The aim of science is the discovery of truth; while the aim of literature is the production of pleasure; and the two aims are not merely distinct but often incompatible, so that large departments of literature are also departments of lying. Not only so, but man is generally more of a pleasure-seeker than a truth-seeker, and the literary spirit, if once admitted to communion with the scientific, will even tend to encroach upon its domain.'[1]

The hedonistic—it might even be said the 'vicious' characteristics of the Georgian theory of a liberal education could not have been more unmercifully exposed; a sharper contrast between the high seriousness of scholarship and the deceitful self-indulgence of literature is hard to imagine; and perhaps it took a poet to do it. Housman's inaugural lecture concludes a development that began when the ideal of new knowledge was incorporated into the Victorian universities, reformed and new, in the final decades of the nineteenth century. Not only was the study of literature inadequate for moral purposes, as Nettleship thought, or lacking critical methods of accuracy and objectivity, as Freeman claimed, but it was detrimental to the entire spirit of modern scholarship and to the moral integrity of the university. Literature was not an imitation of reality, a copy of the steadfast or the abiding in the universe. It represented only the temporary and the mutable. The final implication for liberal education of the research ideal as understood by the nineteenth century was that literature could not and should not serve as the basis or even as one means of a humanistic education. The irony here is unavoidable. Having once excluded science from liberal education, literature in turn found itself excluded by scientific method. From this difficult position the teaching of literary criticism as a fully academic subject has had to slowly extricate itself in the twentieth century, and that is partly why literary critics have taken the leading role in the 'two cultures' debate of recent memory.

Numerous theories and views competed with one another,

[1] 'A. E. Housman's Cambridge Inaugural', *Times Literary Supplement* (9 May 1968), 476–7.

and many educational rivalries were carried on in the six or seven decades following the appearance of the first royal commission reports on the English universities. But finally a new centre was found and a new justification for liberal education. The defining characteristic of liberal education was not that it was broad, not that it directly prepared one for living in the world, and not even that it taught self-restraint. Education was liberal if it enabled the recipient to locate and recognize truth. A relief to the schoolmen of England who had searched long for a replacement for Georgian values, this solution inevitably opened up further philosophical problems, postponing their resolution, however, indefinitely.

13

The Academic Role

IDEALS OF scholarship arriving from the Continent were instrumental in restoring pride to the average Oxbridge don, long demoralized by having an insufficient amount of work to do and depressed by such restrictions as the celibacy clauses attached to fellowships. Fellowships were only technically college appointments. The conditions of tenure actually had nothing to do with teaching or scholarship. The award was a prize, and since the role model for a fellow was not academic, few objected to its being enjoyed away from the university. The fellow rarely aspired to be a scholar or a scientist or a professor. The highest achievements for a person of university education were outside the institutions. It was certainly more prestigious to be the headmaster of a great public school than to be a don, or to become a bishop or a judge. The ultimate honour was cabinet office.

Between 1850 and 1870 a profound role crisis developed within Oxford and Cambridge, bringing into the open questions of career choice, self-esteem, and social status. The crisis was started by the realization that English society was no longer dominated by the values of a landed aristocracy, and that the unofficial yet solid connection between Oxford and Cambridge and the aristocratic-governed State and Church was about to be broken. Pressure for reform was applied in two forms: from Parliament, which threatened to produce greater changes than it actually accomplished, and from undergraduate admissions into the universities on a scale never before experienced. Clearly, a reorientation was required and a complete rethinking of academic roles and university purposes. In this setting the revival of learning—to use one of the slogans of the period—opened up the possibilities of a calling.[1]

The fellowship system had to be the target, for most of the endowments that could be used for education were tied up in special trusts. Demands that the fellowship system be overhauled had been made periodically—in the late eighteenth century, for example, and in the 1830s; but what was consistently absent, besides pressure from Parliament, were a sense of urgency and an ideological element. It was one thing to request the end to celibacy restrictions or geographical quotas, or to insist that holy orders be eliminated as a condition for the life tenure of fellowships, and quite another to require that fellowships released in this way be used for teaching and learning. That is why the ideals associated with the knowledge revolution made a difference. They provided an emotional dynamic in the service of reform, the conviction of a mission or a religious conversion; advocates came close to proclaiming the advent of a millennium. With education reunited to its true purposes, after so many years of wasted efforts and trivial ends, national resolve was bound to be strengthened and national achievement was certain to follow. We now recognize these claims as overdone, and perhaps over-statement could not be avoided as sides were being drawn, but the grand objectives do adequately express the faith of the nineteenth century in the power of education to provide culture, recover moral integrity, and produce, in the long run, a better life for society. By 1880 the necessary changes had been effected. The career academician emerged at Oxford and Cambridge, as he had emerged elsewhere in England, as the dominant type of univer-sity person. The fear of melancholy which had so worried the Georgians was removed once and for all by a new work ethic, and since it was now legitimate for dons to apply themselves to specialized reading or laboratory research, there was no need to worry about the charge of pedantry. Aided by the liberation of fellowships from historic restrictions and also by the establish-ment of new university teaching positions, the numbers of teachers active in the universities increased rapidly. In the decade following 1876, the Oxbridge university staff alone doubled, and throughout the colleges more fellows were en-

[1] See Sheldon Rothblatt, *The Revolution of the Dons* (London and New York, 1968), Part II.

gaged in the task of tuition than had been the case in centuries.

Initially, the most conspicuous influence of the revival of learning was on teaching. The renewed interest in character formation theory at the college level stimulated young dons, leading them to seek out promising undergraduates whose values they might influence. The ideal of universal knowledge also carried with it a heavy teaching commitment, since it was, at one level, an answer to the problem of premature subject concentration. Classical teaching was too often dull and repetitive, 'pedantic and meagre', and the ideal of universal knowledge held out the promise of a new, elevated view of the interconnectedness of learning. Insofar as all scholars were agreed that disciplining the faculties must remain the proximate end of education, universal knowledge at least made clear why this was so, giving the student an ultimate goal to aim for. Universal knowledge was also supposed to be instrumental. It was addressed to what its exponents considered the broadest problems of their generation.

The royal commissioners of the 1850s had definitely been interested in improving the teaching at Oxford and Cambridge. This was, in fact, their primary purpose. Parents whose sons pushed enrolment figures to unprecedented levels in the 1860s were certainly interested in the quality of Oxbridge teaching, especially in view of its extraordinary expense. The costs of university residence were much too high, partly because of the social pressures undergraduates exerted upon one another—a pattern of spending for conspicuous consumption started in the preceding centuries by extravagant scions of noble families— and partly because of the prevalence of private teaching. Everyone knew that the assistance of coaches in passing examinations was indispensable, but the solution was a simple one. The colleges could easily absorb coaching if more fellows were employed in teaching. The need to pay large extra amounts for collegiate instruction when basic tuition costs were already exorbitant seemed an anomaly, an old regime abuse surviving into an age of progress. A generation of parents in a society which had undergone historic reforms in its systems of economic production and political representation and had made changes in the structure of local government and in the character of public administration did not wish to see its standard of living eroded by needless educational expense.

The central objective of the first movements to reform the universities was certainly teaching. It was what that famous academic Tory, Cardinal Newman, wanted, a teaching university, a place for teaching universal knowledge, as he defined it in his famous lectures. This was nearly as true for the professoriate in general, for that part of the university faculty supposedly committed to the task of advancing knowledge in the several fields of scholarship and science, as it was for the collegial fellowship. Halford Vaughan was an exception. He saw no reason why a professor should have to teach or even reside in a university when his object was original learning, but this was assuredly a minority viewpoint. The great Oxbridge professors of the mid-Victorian period are as famous, perhaps more famous, for their teaching as for their contributions to the advance of knowledge. Seeley and Sidgwick at Cambridge, Jowett and T. H. Green at Oxford, were as intensely interested in teaching as in original scholarship. Seeley was, in fact, more interested in teaching, although of a special kind. Jowett saw no fundamental difference in the functions performed by professors and tutors; both were essentially teachers.[1]

In mid-Victorian Oxbridge the professorial system and the collegiate or tutorial system were mutually supporting. Even more, the reinvigoration and expansion of professorial teaching were vital to the success of the awakened collegiate system. For a professorship now became the capstone of an academic career and thus an incentive. The professoriate was necessary to the fellowship, allowing the fellow to become a career teacher, something he had not been for centuries, thus stopping the drain of so many excellent minds into occupations outside the university.

The teaching solution adopted at Oxford and Cambridge, while historically significant, was not in all respects novel. The professor as teacher was the British tradition. It was true of the Scottish professors, who throughout the eighteenth and well into the nineteenth centuries wrote distinguished books on philosophy and the social sciences and gave lectures to undergraduates of secondary school age. As the new English universities of the nineteenth century were founded, beginning with University

[1] Report of the Royal Commission on Durham University, Parliamentary Papers 1863, XLVI. Evidence, 95.

College, London, in the late 1820s, it was the professorial rather than the tutorial system that was adopted, Durham being an exception. The professorial system was far cheaper for students and parents, as no special provision for residence and individual tutoring had to be made and no expensive buildings and gardens had to be maintained in order to create an appropriate atmosphere. Character, if it was to be shaped at all, was shaped intellectually in the classroom. All that was required for the professorial system were lecture halls where large numbers of students could crowd. Furthermore, professorial income could be pegged to attendance, as it often was in Germany, a decision that could, however, and frequently did cause financial hardship, dampening educational innovation and driving some professors out of the universities in search of new patrons, new clientele, and sources of supplementary income. Nevertheless, professorial teaching was the answer for institutions of limited endowments.

The renewed interest in teaching produced some interesting discussions in the mid-Victorian period and later on the relationship of the teacher to his subject of study and the relationship of both to the student. Two positions or models developed. In the first, the teacher was regarded as more important than the subject he taught. This was called the Christian or saintly model, of which charisma in the explicit Weberian meaning was a prime characteristic. The Christian teacher inspired students by his example, by the right conduct visible in his own life. He was in touch with values beyond the banality of everyday life, or he lived those values universally recognized but not universally observed. Knowledge was important insofar as it awakened an interest in values, but never as important as the values themselves. Learning for its own sake was secondary. This model and its variations had obvious uses in those theories of liberal education concerned with character formation.

In the second model the teacher was looked upon as subordinate to his subject; ego gave way to the discipline, personality to knowledge. This was the Socratic model, based upon a characteristic nineteenth-century tendency to identify Socrates with the man described in Plato's dialogues and to read into the characterization an interpretation not supported by the facts. The Socratic model of the teacher soon became identified with the German conception of a professor as someone who imparted scientific

method or the scientific spirit. The great Manchester chemist
Henry Roscoe, who had studied under Bunsen at Heidelberg,
cited him as an example of the true teacher and scientist humbled
by a sense of the limits of his knowledge, his allegiance always
to the subject and never to himself. 'His modesty was natural and
in no degree assumed. In his lectures, when giving an account
of some discovery he had made, or some new apparatus or method
of work which he had instigated, I never heard him mention
himself. It was always "man hat dies gesunden," or "es hat sich
so herausgestellt." In his old age, and looking back on his life-
work, he writes me that he "feels as keenly as ever how modest
and contemptibly small is the amount which I have added to the
building of Science." '[1] One is reminded of Droysen's famous
statement about history. When the facts speak for themselves,
the teacher has merely to present them.

The Socratic model was reinforced in the nineteenth century
by social science determinism, by the belief in impersonal forces
and inevitable cycles or laws of historical movement. The individual was powerless to effect change: he could only understand it, and, at most, clarify its inevitable direction. In the
Socratic model personality characteristics were secondary,
competence and training foremost. As Sir Walter Raleigh said in
1911, using the Socratic model in connection with his own
subject, literary criticism, 'The vanity of teaching . . . often
tempteth a man to forget that he is a blockhead. . . . In our time
we make fuller and more settled provision for teaching. But
learning is still the real business, and the most that a teacher can
do is to help with sympathy and advice those who are travelling
the same way with him.'[2]

It is clear from the remarks of Bunsen in science and Raleigh
in literature that in the course of the nineteenth century one part
of the renewed interest in the teaching of undergraduates began
to separate and attach itself to the research ideal. The Socratic
model was the link between the teaching revolution and the
knowledge revolution, and the person who regarded himself as
the scholar or scientist had to be prepared to recognize the
autonomy of his subject. 'The spirit of learning,' said Raleigh,

[1] Sir Henry Enfield Roscoe, *Life and Experiences* (London and New
York, 1906), 47.
[2] Walter Raleigh, *The Meaning of a University* (Oxford, 1911), 17-18.

'is a good and humble thing, much better than the spirit of teaching.'[1] Increasingly, the whole question of the personal inspiration of the teacher, as well as his moral conduct, the example he as an individual was supposed to set, raised by the notion of the teacher as saint, diminished in importance as the ideal of advancing knowledge spread throughout the international university world. It remained an important consideration for undergraduates, for whom the years after the age of eighteen were still important for self-exploration. But for the scholars and scientists who were at work altering the fundamental precepts of liberal education, the teacher as saint was the wrong model. It drew attention away from learning to self, increasing personal arrogance and simplifying the problem of the place of knowledge in an industrial and scientific world. Theologians were as unattracted to the saintly model as other scholars. As the Dean of the Faculty of Theology in the University of London said in 1911 when he advocated the creation of an 'ideal' or research university in London, 'You must make provision for chairs . . . , not merely for the sake of the students of the University, but for the good name of the University itself. It is not merely the business of a professor to be lecturing and teaching, perhaps elementary work to students, it is also his business to carry on the work of research.'[2]

At the very centre of the knowledge revolution was *Lehrnfreiheit*, the unrestricted pursuit of truth, which meant that some teachers were free to innovate and others devoted themselves to preserving the traditional learning; but for either group intellectual freedom was the most precious ornament of academic life. This had not been the situation earlier, when dons were dismissed from their fellowships or tutorships for advocating unorthodox views on the religion of the Church of England. Academic freedom bore some relationship to the Georgian independence ideal that had emerged in London towards the end of the eighteenth century, but it was really closer to what the Victorians considered the essence of professional behaviour. Georgian independence was basically independence from some person or group; it was much closer to being a 'liberty'. It did

[1] Ibid.
[2] Report of the Royal Commission on University Education in London, Parliamentary Papers 1911 (Cd. 5911), XX, 500.

not imply duties or responsibilities to be given in return for independence. It was primarily a status to be enjoyed. The Victorian conception of professional independence incorporated a service ideal. Education was the foundation of the service, although exactly what service to provide and how to provide it caused academicians as much difficulty as did the definition and meaning of a liberal education.

We must not exaggerate the degree of discipline specialization or expertise implied by the phrase 'professionalism'. Certainly in the first instance, the knowledge revolution did not automatically mean the emergence of the expert, whether in government, industry, or the universities. There are degrees of professionalism as there are degrees of amateurism. A simple contrast does not really give us the historical condition we may seek. In the early Victorian period Edwin Chadwick considered himself an authority in the area of public health, yet he had nothing but contempt for medical men. In the field of epidemiology he was mainly influenced by the theories of civil engineers. Before the physician could be respected as an expert in questions of community sanitation, it was necessary for him to upgrade his professional qualifications, a situation that did not occur in England until after the 1860s. Even then it was possible to find leading government bureaucrats who may have been trained physicians, but who otherwise showed very little competence, or perhaps even basic interest, in public medicine or in the control of contagious diseases. In the second half of the nineteenth century, the school inspectors employed in the Department of Education were likely to be highly intelligent, efficient, and conscientious, but also without any special competence or experience in the administration of mass education. Their qualification was limited to a first-class degree from Oxford or Cambridge and a friend or acquaintance in the Department. Unquestionably, the cream of the Oxford honours schools or the Cambridge tripos were an improvement over the aristocrats and their cousins who controlled the civil service departments before 1850, but we must not overstate the degree of specialized education or special qualification required for one group to gradually replace another. In fact, the first phase of the knowledge revolution as represented by university persons such as the Mark Pattison of 1850 was an attempt to get away from specialism, which was seen to be the principal barrier to the creation of a vital liberal arts syllabus.

In the last decades of the nineteenth century the specialist ideal, which had already established itself in the newer universities, began to influence Oxbridge as well. Of course, some Oxbridge dons of 1900 still congratulated themselves on resisting the fragmentation of learning and praised one another for upholding the principles of general education. But the issues in which the question of a liberal education was sometimes raised indicate that the protagonists no longer possessed an unmistakable idea of the suitable forms of liberal instruction. In 1905, for example, a large number of tutors and lecturers protested against the plan of the Regius Professor to introduce a thesis essay based on original sources into the syllabus of the Oxford History School. A thesis existed as part of the history curriculum at Manchester, where the Regius Professor had been trained; but the dons argued that it would introduce an undesirable professional element into what was 'a liberal education through history'. Examinations, however, they regarded as well within the spirit of liberal arts teaching.[1]

The trend, nevertheless, was towards specializing and contributing to original research. A teaching knowledge of a subject was becoming insufficient as a test of professional competence. More was required. Even the long-standing belief that a practising—an acclaimed—London barrister was qualified to be a professor of law or a legal historian without also being a seriously-trained legal scholar was challenged in university circles. In 1886, when he was elected to the Downing Professorship of the Laws of England at Cambridge, Maitland raised the question with customary wit: 'My own belief to the last moment was that some Q.C. who was losing health or practice would ask for the place and get it.[2] If not every university subject had become professionally academic as we now understand the phrase, requiring an advanced degree in the subject or other proof of research competence, and if there was still room in English academic life for the man of general education who had achieved

[1] A. T. Milne, 'History at the Universities: Then and Now', in *History*, LIX (February, 1974), 40.

[2] C. H. S. Fifoot, *Frederic William Maitland, A Life* (Cambridge, Mass., 1971), 92.

some eminence outside the university, there can be no doubt that this form of amateurism was becoming deeply resented. In the same year that Maitland received his appointment to the Downing chair, the famous Victorian churchman and sometime Headmaster of Harrow, Henry Montagu Butler, was named Master of Trinity College, Cambridge, a position in the gift of the crown. One of the greatest Cambridge men of his generation, Henry Sidgwick, confessed himself depressed and dissatisfied 'at the snub given to academic work' by Butler's appointment. Sidgwick liked him personally. They had been together at the university, and Butler was a serious and important man. But he was not a scholar, had made no contributions to the advance of learning, and, consequently, in Sidgwick's eyes was not a professional academic person.[1]

As long as universal knowledge was the goal of many prominent and serious members of the academic community, it was still possible to have learned amateurs in the university world, but by the end of the nineteenth century, as the great comprehensive *summas* and positivist theories of social development became less interesting and valuable to scholars, as the newer universities registered real advances in the solution of scientific and technological problems, the model of the man of general education was being superseded. While a grand philosophical overview was still important in the minds of some scholars and likely to appear as the stated objective of specialties still in the process of definition, most academics associated intellectual achievement with narrower areas of concentration.[2] The growth in the number of fields, subjects, and specialties that are the rule of the university today can be followed throughout the second half of the nineteenth century and into the twentieth century. It is easy to appreciate the excitement so often expressed in biographies, testimonies, and addresses and lectures of the period. It is no wonder that the life of the mind was so highly praised when learning appeared fresh and endless, when the terrifying

[1] Arthur Sidgwick and Eleanor M. Sidgwick, *Henry Sidgwick, A Memoir* (London, 1906), 460–1.
[2] For a summary of the two positions, plus an excellent review of the issues involved in the creation of modern academic associations, see the materials collected by the Sociological Society entitled *Sociological Papers* (London, 1905), British Museum Ac 2263.

applications of science to weaponry had not yet stunned the imaginations of men and women, when ideas of racial or national superiority had not yet been legitimized in Europe by academic decree, and when theories of the absurd had not penetrated the culture and education of western civilization.

Specialism fragmented the university world as it had never been fragmented before. The official scholastic curriculum of the seventeenth century, although it was supplemented by a revolution in scientific thinking, had imposed a unity on the educational life of the university and defined an overall purpose to study. The recovering university of the early nineteenth century had concentrated on a select number of subjects and carefully ordered the priority given to other subjects. The expansion in the number of fields after 1850, the establishment of new chairs, and the revival of the professional schools ended whatever educational unity had hitherto existed. Seen in this perspective, the universal knowledge ideal was both the last attempt to unify the educational purpose of the university and the first phase of the process that destroyed the unity.

Specialism became essential to academic professionalism and to professionalism generally as it had not been in the eighteenth century. To be sure, there was a professional movement of substantial proportions in the Georgian period, but its primary objective was not competence itself but competence as validated by status. Georgian writers, architects, painters, and physicians were more interested in their social standing than in their reputations as professional men. Status professionalism developed in a society where style and manners were co-determinants of prestige, and prestige was more important than career. As this was the case, career preparation through university education was essentially unnecessary. A university education would have been important only if it had been solidly based on the ideal of the gentleman so closely associated with rank and position. As we have seen, it failed to fulfil this requirement.

Unlike status professionalism, occupational professionalism, Victorian in origin, depends upon competence as validated by the diploma; but this is only one guarantee that the professional man has been adequately trained. In addition, the association of professional men, highly organized and self-regulating, determines both the educational criteria and the working ethics

184

of the profession. Merit as defined by the association and guaranteed by the university is more important than social standing, which, if it is achieved at all, is achieved through distinction in the profession. Career is foremost, and general education by itself is insufficient to guarantee success.

Occupational professionalism and specialism, although they did not necessarily originate together, soon joined. At the core of the union was the professionalization of academic life. Since it was the specialty that provided the academic person with his self-assurance and his success, it was in his interest both to advance his subject and to enlarge its general importance. The accomplishment of this took various forms, depending upon the nature of the subject. New constituencies and new audiences were created, as they were created in Georgian times, and new alignments between academic persons and non-academic communities appeared.

The civic universities are an excellent example of this process of professional growth. From the start, the newer universities were closely identified with the manufacturing industries of the Midlands and the North. 'The thrust bearing lubrication, colliery pumps, vanadium steels, chrome leather, gas fires, sparking plugs, and radio tuning all owed much to the work of the professors while products like cheese, soap, beer and the quadruple expansion engine were all considerably improved by their work.'[1] This pattern of involvement, while to continue past 1914, underwent various alterations. As some industries developed their own research facilities, the civic universities gave more attention to projects that can be called pure research.

Initially, Oxbridge regarded the connections between the newer universities and the industrial regions of England with distrust and disdain. Although Cambridge professors in the early Victorian period had worked in several government-sponsored research projects, they had refrained from offering their services to the new manufacturing districts. Of course, it must be added that in the earlier period industry had not developed to the point where university research of any kind was useful in production. Industry returned the disdain, and it continued into the later Victorian period and well into the

[1] Michael Sanderson, *The Universities and British Industry 1850–1970* (London, 1972), 93.

twentieth century. By and large, the great scientific achievements of Cambridge—the discoveries in atomic physics that took place at the Cavendish Laboratory, for example—had no connection whatsoever with industrial enterprise. As long as dons were able to develop their specialties without substantial monetary assistance from outside, they could mock the new universities and freely indulge their wit.

> He gets degrees in making jam
> At Liverpool and Birmingham.[1]

But already in the Victorian period there were important signs of malaise. It was sensed, particularly, but not exclusively, by representatives of newer subjects, that the historical conditions allowing Oxbridge complete supremacy in higher education were passing, and that a new effort at accommodation between the ancient universities and important interests outside was necessary. During the first world war the sharp donnish distinction between applied and pure research disappeared in the interests of patriotism and national survival.

Specialization was both a cause and a consequence of the diversification of academic life in the second half of the nineteenth century. Or to explain it another way, it is not absolutely clear that interest in an academic specialty in every case preceded its professional development. Other variables were important—the availability of academic employment, for example. The German case, whereby chairs in new disciplines were sometimes established because the professorial system closed off academic mobility, is well known. The acceptance of a new subject into the university world, whether in Germany or in England, was not automatic. Despite the belief that knowledge must advance and that innovation was essential to the continued vitality of a university, academics zealously guarded their areas of influence. Recognition had to be fought for, sometimes in bitter competition

---

[1] Ibid., 93–5. Lord Ashby has commented on the important change in the relations of the new Victorian universities and their lay governing councils. The latter were supposed to guarantee some kind of interplay between industry, commerce, local public life, and the universities; but in time initiative came solely from inside the universities, and the influence from outside dissipated. See A. C. Crombie, ed., *Scientific Change* (London, 1963), 727.

with established fields. Specific goals had to be elaborated, financial support obtained, positions acquired, a place in the curriculum, in the library, or in the laboratory to be found. Efforts had to be made to enlist the interests of students and obtain other forms of public support. Publicity and advertizing became necessary, and large claims were sometimes made on behalf of young subjects in order to assure their support and survival. The history of the university in the past hundred years is certainly a wonderful account of new ideas and discoveries, but it is also an account of academic manoeuvring on a new scale. It is to a considerable extent the history of precisely those professional or pedagogical associations that arose to defend and promote developing academic or occupational interests. The internal histories of all universities have been profoundly affected by the growth of professional associations. The collegiate structure, because it is mainly, if not solely, used for teaching, has been the most successful in resisting the implications of specialism, although it, too, ultimately derives its academic direction from the faculty boards and from the examination system.

The growth of professional associations generally between 1850 and 1900 was an extraordinary development. In 1850 they were comparatively rare. There were naturally philosophical and literary societies within the universities and journal publications. But the number of such groups was limited, and their place in both university life and in the development of academic specialism was not significant. When in the 1850s dons testified before the royal commissions investigating the teaching, discipline, and finance of the ancient universities, they usually did so as individuals. The one single important group to appear in the 1850s was the Oxford Tutors' Association, which lobbied successfully for college teaching, but the Oxford Tutors' Association was not, strictly speaking, a professional organization. Its task was not to certify skills, but to defend an interest within one single academic institution. The same was true of another pressure group composed of professors which formed in opposition to the tutors. By the end of the century the number of groups, academic interests, associations, and specialties that could be expected to testify before a government commission or committee of inquiry was staggering. When the reorganization of the University of London was considered at the end of the nineteenth century and the beginning of the twentieth, representatives of medical and legal associations, of hospitals, colleges, and schools all came forward to present their views on liberal and professional education, as did ad hoc groups formed to represent teachers of different income and status categories, field workers in social science subjects, and representatives from architectural firms. Throughout England, business, industry, and even local government began to take an interest in the work of university-trained professionals.

Specialism and professionalism account for changes in the development of the modern university which appear as contradictions. Specialism produced differentiation within the university, complicated its structure of governance, and changed academic roles. The development of the academic career gave university scholars and scientists a greater interest in the internal affairs of their institutions than they were allowed to have in the days of the Oxbridge prize fellowship system and the non-resident professor. Interests were turned inward to the institution, as they had once been forced outwards away from it. But at the same time, the organization of specialists into professional associations, arranging national and international meetings, sponsoring special projects, publishing journals and newsletters, created an extended university community such as had not existed in principle since the Middle Ages. Specialism also enabled academic persons to look outwards from their institutions by involving them in the many activities of an enormously complex industrial society, voracious in its demands for new skills and proficiencies.

It is a paradox of the modern university that while the number and level of its contacts to outside communities have vastly increased through the activity of its members, its overall size, internal differentiation, and international character, its involvement in administration, teaching, and research has given it a complete self-absorption. University faculties feel little need for the kind of social contacts yearned for by isolated Georgian dons. Unless there are some compelling institutional reasons to do so—usually fund-raising in some form or public relations—the average university teacher is content to remain with his peers. Whatever the necessity for outside contacts, they rarely have anything to do with career or personal advancement except in the most remote and indirect sense. The modern university faculty member has his professional identification, his standing in the community of scholarship and science, and his special institutional affiliation; but he has no social model in the narrow sense on which to form himself. He knows of no single outside reference group as important to him as the gentlemen of Georgian England were indispensable to the monks and pedants of Oxford and Cambridge. The importance of this change for the history of a liberal education is that 'getting-along' has ceased to be a social problem for dons, even if 'getting-on' remains.

Yet another paradox of the modern English university (or, for that matter, Scottish and American ones) is the degree to which it has been able to balance its internal values against outside interests. A high degree of intellectual autonomy co-exists with numerous obligations to groups outside—to government, to industry, to the professions, to broadcasting, and to journalism. The contemporary university has been able to assume a primary place in modern social and economic life which the Georgian university could not, and it has been able to do this without developing or trying to develop shared intellectual or social values with the rest of society. This is a point certainly worth remembering when the university is denounced for being completely the servant of the State or subservient to the dominant economic interests within it.

Yet despite the great degree of intellectual freedom existing within universities, it is unduly optimistic to conclude that conflicts affecting the intellectual autonomy and self-governing status of universities do not exist and will not exist. By no means is the modern university absolute master in its own kingdom. Not even the University Grants Committee of the Treasury, representing as it mainly does the academic community, is a perfect guarantor of university independence. Any time an educational institution assumes or is forced to assume relationships with influential bodies outside itself, questions affecting the priority of studies within the university and the values professed by it inevitably arise. Decision-making is then to some extent shared, especially if money is involved. But to speak for a moment only of yesterday, it is certain that one great historical achievement of the past century has been the extent to which scholars and scientists have been able to choose their subjects and develop them largely through professional control of the content. If research problems did not always originate within the universities, certainly methods for solving the problems were developed there and new projects and lines of inquiry started.

Academic professionalism, original research, the new involvement with outside institutions inevitably created a basic change not only in the concept of liberal education, but also in the whole function or purpose of a university, in what Newman, adapting Coleridge, had called its 'idea'. Of course, that 'idea' was closely related to the type of education provided within the university, and so it had been customary to view the university as a liberal arts institution. It was common in the early nineteenth century to regard the university as always having been a liberal arts institution and to deny that it had ever had any other rival purpose. 'The most ancient part of the University of Paris was the faculty of arts or philosophy,' wrote a don in 1835. In his view the *trivium* and *quadrivium* were no less than the twin pillars of a liberal education, conveniently corresponding to the philology and mathematics taught at Oxford and Cambridge. 'The original functions of a University were those of a "school of arts", out of which the three professional faculties were subsequently developed. It was a *studium generale*, and could send forth *sophistae generales*, and *magistri artium*, with reference only to the acknowledged elements of a liberal education, and without any regard to the professional destination of its students.'[1]

It was precisely at the turn of the century that the historian and theologian Hastings Rashdall challenged and overturned this long-standing conclusion regarding the origins of the university. He argued—and his viewpoint has prevailed—that professional education had always been the distinguishing characteristic of the university. In his monumental study of the European university and in the lectures he gave around the kingdom, he publicized his findings in an obvious effort to promote support for a university ideal with which he was completely in accord. No longer was it improper for universities to relate their education directly to careers or to train their students for specific professional occupations, as in fact they had long been doing. There

[1] Quoted in John William Donaldson, *Classical Scholarship and Classical Learning* (Cambridge, 1856), 20, 25.

had always been some attempt by someone to twist the strands of a liberal education round some honourable career. A correct understanding of the origins of the European university showed that this was the only proper course. The Rashdall view legitimated the developing situation—the new idea for a university—by giving an historical explanation for it. He used historical method, as others of his generation were using it, to trace the origins of institutions in order to clarify the meaning of their development, and the message was clear: polite education and character formation were later and undesirable accretions.

Once career preparation was seen to be the true purpose of a university education, one of the oldest hurdles in the history of liberal education could be surmounted. General education was unnecessary if there were so many occupations in society for which a university education could prepare undergraduates. Why should university faculties trouble themselves over a definition of education that put them in the awkward position of having to identify those occupations appropriate for a university-educated person and those not? Why be jesuitical? A veil was lifted, as Professor Dale of University College, London, had tried to lift it in the early nineteenth century when he said there were no differences between liberal and professional forms of education.[1] He was roundly criticized. And yet the problem was not so easily resolved, for perhaps there had been a point to the defence of liberal education through the centuries and possibly there remained a lesson worth considering even in a mature, industrial society. A disquieting sense of a lost and valued principle continued to trouble the minds of academicians, even as they struggled to eliminate traditional categories and ideas from their understanding of the purposes of a liberal education. Some of the difficulties involved in accepting Rashdall's discovery are beautifully illustrated in a report issued by the University Grants Committee on 3 February 1921:

'There is indeed no inherent antagonism between a liberal and vocational training,' the report began, continuing with the Rashdall conclusion: 'Universities began in mediaeval times as groups of teachers and students devoted to the study of some profession, and since a large number of students in the depart-

[1] Thomas Dale, *An Introductory Lecture* (London, 1828), 8.

ments of the Arts and Pure Science Faculties of a modern University enter the teaching profession, their University training is in a sense as vocational as that of students taking courses with more directly utilitarian applications.' Here the committee was guilty of adopting a common fallacy. Because students will use their education for entry into a particular occupation does not mean the education they received is designed with that job in mind. As if to recognize the fallacy, the committee then contrasted the arts and pure sciences courses with subjects 'more directly utilitarian', although another qualifying sentence immediately followed: 'It is clearly impossible to draw a hard and fast line between pure theory and practical application.' Not wishing to abandon the attempt completely, however, the committee then resorted to a traditional definition: 'The difference between a liberal and vocational training lies not so much in the subject studied as in the spirit in which it is pursued. What is essential is to maintain that breadth and proportion of view which are implied by a University standpoint.' Yet further on in the same report, the requirement of breadth was gently nudged aside, still struggling, as specialization, the antithesis of breadth, was eased into its place. 'The bases on which all Applied Science is founded are ever broadening as the boundaries of knowledge are extended,' the committee observed. 'It follows that University courses must tend to become increasingly exacting if they are to be continuously informed with fundamental scientific principles.' No fundamental literary principles, but fundamental scientific principles. It is true that the phrase 'increasingly exacting' need not be, strictly speaking, tied to specialization, but that is certainly the overall drift and context of the report. The entire discussion is far away in 'spirit' from what the Georgians believed the nature of a liberal education to be, and not at all what they would have understood as 'that breadth and proportion of view which are implied by a University standpoint.'[1]

The report is a characteristic document of the twentieth century, an unsuccessful attempt to combine principles of education which were once certainly antithetical and still do not reconcile easily. A reluctance to abandon the past forces the

[1] Report of the University Grants Committee, 3 February 1921, 10.

ideas of yesterday to dress in uncomfortable and unsuitable clothes. Over and over again we can notice the same attempt by scholars and scientists and men and women of ideas to define liberal education by joining principles and values that at bottom have different historical origins and acutely different cultural meanings and purposes.[1]

Surveying the course of university history from 1914, a twentieth-century Georgian would have noticed an enormous change in the influence exerted over education in general, over the professions, and over government by English universities. Never since the mid seventeenth century had they been so important, and never had their relationships with so many other

---

[1] But to be fair, it must be reiterated that the muddle is as much Victorian as twentieth-century. See the address by the Professor of Greek at St. Andrews entitled *The End of Liberal Education* (Edinburgh, 1868). His argument bounces back and forth from character formation to 'an increased perception of the inward power and freedom of the human spirit', to cultivating intellect, to the 'simple love of truth', and to finding 'the highest form under which we ourselves and this universe, and the Great First Cause, and the relation of each to all, may be most perfectly conceived'.

The recent symposium on higher education in the United States arranged by *Daedalus* (Fall, 1974) certainly proves that American efforts to define liberal education are vexed and uncertain. It also illustrates how universal is the tendency to extract specific educational ideals and values from confining historical contexts. For example, in the course of one essay, Martin Meyerson, President of the University of Pennsylvania, moves through almost all the customary attributes and purposes of liberal instruction as if ambiguities do not exist. Liberal education is equated with breadth, with being 'flexible, civilized, and responsible', with learning for its own sake, with the 'analytic method that has been the ideal of the arts and sciences', with humane objectives and with a life of service united to a calling. Meyerson goes on to repeat the common opinion that 'Humanistic and scientific learning have been divorced. In the eighteenth and nineteenth centuries science was seen as part of the humanistic achievements of man, a liberating force. Now science is confused with technology and is sometimes viewed by humanists as a threat to the values of our culture.' If my own argument is correct, this view has to be substantially qualified, at least for England. I have also been suggesting that the omnibus ideals commonly associated with liberal education are contradictory in historical terms and are more than the tradition can bear, whether in England or elsewhere. This is not to say that they are unworthy but to question the possibility of their realization in our own time.

G   193

institutions been so involved and far-reaching. The examination system, which had been one of the great changes of the early nineteenth century, gave the universities *de facto* control over the curriculum of the secondary schools through school-leaving and scholarship examinations, and over higher education in general through the university extra-mural teaching movements and the local examinations. The schools periodically rebelled against this power, demanding showdown conferences to resolve outstanding differences, but once established, the benevolent tyranny remained. Through examinations the future elite was drawn out of the secondary schools into the universities, and the standard of high school education generally was maintained nationally. What existed in 1900 or 1914 had not existed in 1650 or in 1750, 1800 or in 1850: educational systems organized on a national scale providing instruction for hundreds of thousands of children and young persons at least through elementary school and for many of them through secondary school, all orchestrated from above by a number of government departments whose members were recruited from the universities, particularly from Oxbridge. And the lever which moved this mass was the belief in the supremacy of the discipline and in the autonomy of the subject. It was quite out of the question to rank subjects according to either their intrinsic worth or their utility. What was important was scientific method. No matter what the subject, it could be treated scientifically. Scientific modes of comprehension were the essence of any kind of education, whether liberal or professional, whether in medicine, metallurgy, business administration, classics, genetics, or in the deciphering of cuneiform tablets.

14

Following the Argument Whithersoever it Goes

The function of the nineteenth century, wrote G. M. Young not too long ago in a memorable example of the retrospective fallacy, for which he may be forgiven (as the same philosophical vice is exhibited here), 'was to disengage the disinterested intelligence'. If ages have such whiggish functions, then the nineteenth century completely disrupted the eighteenth-century idea of a liberal education. However we view that idea—as character formation, as preparation for life, as the acquisition of Taste or particular kinds of knowledge—it has changed beyond recognition in the past hundred and fifty years. The relationship between liberal education and knowledge has had to undergo continual metamorphosis: from the great known or received truths of the eighteenth century, to new knowledge assimilated to old truths, then new knowledge employed to yield new truths and to construct an inclusive philosophical schema. Then liberal education underwent a positivist phase where factual knowledge was stressed, and this in turn produced different ways of organizing facts, 'modes of thinking', ways of arranging information, methods and models which no longer make claims on universal conceptions of order and value.

Each of these phases has bequeathed something to the history of liberal education; no single principle, purpose, or idea associated with some aspect of liberal education has ever been permanently discarded. Yet neither have the contributions been cumulative, forming a new synthetic view of the meaning of a liberal education. Characteristically, they have been competitive. Hence it is possible for a liberal education to be all things to all men. For Pattison, 'The perfect education consists in the perfection and enlargement of the intellect *per se.*'[1] For Roscoe in 1874 the perfection of the intellect was equated with the higher mental development of mankind.[2] Other Victorians made the critical mind the end of a liberal education, and not stopping there, made that synonymous with the highest culture of the nation, and so on, *ad infinitum*. A liberal education can be Truth, Taste, sociability, liberality, humanism, sensitivity, sound critical principles, critical self-awareness, scientific detachment, a glimpse into the permanent realities of existence, civilization, culture—all these have at one historical time or another been identified with the purposes and meaning of a liberal education. Sometimes they were cardinal ends, sometimes means to other ends, sometimes parts of subordinate clauses in sentences drifting away towards other destinations. Sometimes they were concepts only tangential to a particular discussion, sometimes afterthoughts employed for rhetorical effect, familiar slogans to comfort restless audiences. Sometimes they were the shadows cast by a reproving past.

But one meaning of a liberal education has, in fact, assumed priority over all others, and its emergence and rise to supremacy can be followed in the history I have been discussing. It appeared first in Victorian times. It was the result of the knowledge revolution, of the research ideal, of a belief in the power of the intellect, of specialism and professionalism, of the breakdown of the teleological universe and even the positivist universe, and of the disintegration of a traditional confidence in the strength of education to produce a reliable social type. The new meaning of a liberal education that superseded all the others was the search for truth—not abiding truth, but contingent truth, based on facts and sources. In the beginning, scholars and scientists were confident of their ability to find absolute truth, but from an early point there were tensions in the ideal. Meaning could not be derived until all the facts were available; yet as the definition of a 'fact' began to change, it appeared that the task of collection would never end. While this had certain advantages—it justified on-going research—it also produced frustration. To relieve the

[1] Pattison, 433–4.
[2] Henry E. Roscoe, 'Original Research as a Means of Education', in *Essays and Addresses, by Professors and Lecturers of the Owens College, Manchester* (London, 1874), 57.

tension, the ideal had to be modified. Research, or the process of seeking truth, was more important than finding it. And because what is true could not be found, only sought, liberal education had to be the process of training that allowed the search to go on. Liberal education was consequently the exercise of the free intelligence or the critical intelligence, never satisfied, always restless, not comfortable in the presence of platitude. To follow the argument whithersoever it goes was the purpose of a liberal education. A mid-Victorian could even say that—in fact did—but could a Georgian?

Today we have gone so far beyond a world of final causes that even the search for truth has an uncomfortable dimension. The extraordinary explosion of information and proliferation of modes of thinking have made it impossible for any one mind to comprehend but a small portion of what is known. In despair the intellect turns back upon itself, creating its own world of rules and looking for reassurance in heuristic models which it is tempted to substitute for reality. Paradoxically, this is the closest liberal education has ever come to its most elusive historical dream, the belief in the value of knowledge for its own sake. Yet to be tempted in this way is to forsake entirely the original purpose of the humanistic objective in English liberal education: life in the world, education for living with others.

Thus the path from the eighteenth century to the present is an anfractuous one. In time, a liberal education, which once meant repressing one's own desires in order to accommodate others—not exactly, to be sure, self-sacrifice—came to mean the pursuit of knowledge for one's own purposes, for creativity perhaps, or for psychological freedom, despite society if necessary.[1]

---

[1] One difference between mid eighteenth-century and twentieth-century views of the relationship between the individual and society can be illustrated by the example of the picaro or picaroon. The picaro, a potential rebel against society, is never allowed to be permanently estranged by novelists of the period. While he is always an outsider at the beginning of his adventures, he always returns to society at the end. Neither his values nor those of others change in the interim. It is the nature of the picaroon, explains Robert Alter, to remain untouched by experience, to be always as he was. I conclude that the conflict between the individual and Georgian society is therefore merely an appearance and never a reality. It arises because of a misunderstanding or a mistake. Under these circumstances true rebellion is not possible. The picaroon disappears

The academic profession legitimizes the twentieth-century view of truth and sanctions a certain amount of withdrawal as necessary to the life of the mind. Or, as Walter Raleigh put it in his lecture at Aberystwyth in 1911, 'Thought is a lonely business. The life of a man of science, a man of letters, an artist, is essentially a life of much solitude. The very things which make social life pleasant and possible, the things which raise the standard of comfort and civilization, we owe to men who struggled along with their own thoughts in lonely contemplation. . . . [W]e shall be foolish if we forget that we are dependent on the lonely men, whom we cannot command.'[1] But in return for this luxury and as justification for these claims, the profession demands a form of accountability. It creates standards to evaluate the consequences of withdrawal and to measure its achievements. The essential check on this philosophical and psychological development has therefore been a sociological one. It is the profession that now limits residence in the garden of Epicurus.

For the past hundred years the lonely men whom Raleigh described have found a suitable environment for reflection and contemplation in the hermitic cells away from the crowded centres of modern life, where the traffic and worry of the streets outside penetrate with some difficulty. In these places the post-Georgian ideals of a liberal education are followed on the basis of a special but vulnerable understanding with the world outside. Whereas the Georgian critics thought it foolish for a university to be separate from the rest of society, reckless for it to wander an independent course, thereby endangering the mental health of its inhabitants and damaging their personalties, a different view is presently held. It has been accepted, at least until very recently, that while no university can remain apart from society or indifferent to it, universities do perform functions not duplicated elsewhere, foremost among them being the objective evaluation of ideas and institutions. 'Without contemplation,'

---

when the rebel makes his entry as the hero of Holcroft's political novels written towards the end of the eighteenth century. Robert Alter, 'The Picaroon as Fortune's Plaything', in *Essays on the 18th-Century Novel*, ed. Robert Donald Spector (Bloomington, Indiana, 1965); Rodney M. Baine, 'Thomas Holcroft and the Revolutionary Novel', *University of Georgia Monographs*, Number 13 (Athens, Georgia, 1965).

[1] Raleigh, *Meaning of a University*, 19.

said the Provost of University College, London, in a recent television broadcast, 'we will not get really penetrating criticism of men in power, men of the world, slick journalists, trend-setters, and of authorities such as myself. That's what universities exist to provide. As far as I am concerned, they certainly provide it.'[1] We have seen how recent this view of the functions of a university really is.

I have argued for discontinuity in the history of a liberal education in England, but discontinuity does not easily dispose of every historical problem. The phrase 'a liberal education' at least enjoys an extraordinary continuity and has survived each of the revolutions that should have disposed of it. Even today the words continue to exercise a hold on the imagination, and scarcely any educational change of significant proportions is undertaken without reference to some aspect of its history. If the phrase survives, then perhaps it is actually capable of inspiring action, for to name a thing is to give it life.

Perhaps, then, there is a deep underlying continuity in the history of a liberal education in England, and the changes here described have been necessary historical efforts to keep the ideals recurrent. If so, the continuity would be this, that the essence of a liberal education remains what it was in ancient times: the search for a good life, for gardens and islands, happy kingdoms and exalted valleys, and that this is a constant, whether Greek, Georgian, or German. The ends of a liberal education are truly ethical. The Georgian belief in civility, Goethe's trilogy of values, and the modern critical ideal expressed as the search for truth are all different ways of achieving the same goal.[2] Hence the continuity as well of the two necessary conditions for achieving the good life: the belief that before all else liberal education must inculcate reason, from which it follows that a proper

[1] Lord Annan, 'What Are Universities for, Anyway?' in *The Listener* (2 November 1972), 599.
[2] Along such lines argues P. H. Hirst in an interesting presentation. See his 'Liberal Education and the Nature of Knowledge', in *Education and the Development of Reason*, ed. R. F. Dearden *et al.* (London, 1972), 391–414. Hirst's conversational ideal, which he ascribes to Michael Oakshott, suggests the Georgian sociability ideal, although the latter was not built initially or exclusively on intellectual foundations. See also Lord Ashby, 'The Future of the Nineteenth Century Idea of a University', *Minerva*, VI (Autumn, 1967).

education is general or broad; and that it must teach the individual to live in harmony with himself and with the world.

The idea that a liberal education must be a broad or general education and that under no circumstances must it ever be subservient to a specific career, for that would be an 'interested' and not a 'disinterested' use of education, self-serving and not selfless, has caused more difficulty for the theory of a liberal education than perhaps any other aspect. Education conceived in this way has only been possible for a leisured class and at a stage in the evolution of society when expert knowledge was not necessary for the exercise of political and economic leadership. A leisured class—and it must at the same time supply a political elite—can afford the luxury of an education that emphasizes broad principles of leadership and conduct derived from the reading of a few select texts. We have noticed how general or breadth education was actually defined in the Georgian period, how much it was dependent upon non-academic considerations, and how closely it was tied to a particular historical and cultural development. More complex industrial societies with far greater levels of specialization than the Georgians ever knew have difficulty isolating indispensable guiding principles and choosing the syllabus which teaches them.

Yet in several respects the principle of breadth is still alive. Universities today are interested in crossing the boundaries between traditional disciplines and in creating new programmes and combinations of subjects, even while the process of specialty-building continues and new conceptions of expert knowledge appear. Furthermore, while the trend towards greater specialization in university education remains basically uncontested, and liberal education continues to narrow in subject concentration, there has been an opposite trend in vocational education. There the instruction has broadened. Mechanics institutes, art and design classes, mining schools, agricultural programmes, and other institutions founded in the Victorian period to provide practical education for what were called the 'industrious' members of society, moved away in their own century from an exclusively vocational orientation to teach general science and theory as much as practice. The result has been that what were once regarded as servile occupations have been elevated into the ranks of professions, where they have then been brought into the world of university education. Because of this reformation in the teaching of vocational subjects, it has become nearly impossible today to distinguish between various kinds of institutions offering advanced instruction, whether or not they are actually called universities. All of them, whether Oxford and Cambridge, London, Redbrick, Plateglass, the Scottish and Welsh universities, and the colleges of advanced technology, incorporate similar ranges of educational methods and ideals, and offer similar mixtures of liberal and professional forms of education. It can be said that the balance of subjects varies from institution to institution, as does the technical or liberal emphasis, and certainly the quality and appeal of institutions differ enormously.[1] But this does not alter the conclusion that all institutions of advanced education share more educational values than at first they might be inclined to believe. And certainly there are often greater differences between disciplines than there are between single institutions.

There is one group of contemporary writers who agrees with the thrust of the University Grants Committee Report of 1921 that an education can be called liberal if the subjects are taught in their fullest ramifications and illiberal if the focus is limited. They welcome the gradual obliteration of the invidious distinction between liberal and servile education introduced by the Georgians. Vocational education is direct career preparation, that cannot be denied, but career is what nearly all men and women must have; it is the normal condition of life. Therefore, the broadest possible conception of career will furnish exactly that spirit of liberality that has so long been missing from all forms of education.[2] From the point of view of those who believe that breadth is truly a central necessity of liberal education, that education should not be merely useful, this suggestion is heartening, for instructors who teach traditional liberal arts subjects in universities no longer comprise the majority of university-level

[1] In 1968 Oxford and Cambridge were still the first choice of persons already there and those elsewhere wishing to move. The two senior universities therefore continue to 'serve as status and intellectual models' in the British academic world. A. H. Halsey and Martin Trow, *The British Academics* (London, 1971), 230-3.

[2] Eric E. Robinson, *The New Polytechnics* (Harmondsworth, 1968), 92-3.

teachers as they did for centuries. According to the 1968 calculations of A. H. Halsey and Martin Trow, only 16 per cent of
the total number of teachers in British universities represent
arts subjects, while nearly half of all the academics in Britain
are in 'some kind of natural or social science based technology.
The technologist, thus broadly defined, has the most plausible
claim to be thought of as the typical university teacher.'[1]

The gradual disappearance of the barriers between liberal and
vocational education does not gladden everyone, however, for
this development, too, has its detractors. There are those who
regard the broadening of the vocational syllabus under the
influence of ideals of liberal education as too elitist. In their
view, a flourishing tradition of practical education was interrupted in the nineteenth century and deflected from its proper
historical course. They trace the decline of British technology
in the twentieth century directly to the introduction of breadth
ideals and the influence of the principles of pure science, which
represent for them standards of values more appropriate to the
privileged classes of society than to manual workers, and the
result of the mix they consider to be a loss of material benefits
to all sectors of society and a further intensification of class
snobbery in English society.[2]

Quite possibly the non-vocational ideology of a liberal
education has survived—where it has survived—because of the
rise of the modern graduate school in the very late nineteenth
century. Before then, the inns of court and the London teaching
hospitals performed a similar service for liberal education. Because postgraduate education was never expected to be liberal,
it could comfortably assume the task of career preparation.
Undergraduate education in the universities could then safely
remain liberal, provided the liberal arts degree possessed some
standing in the professional schools. If a liberal education
directly qualified a student for a particular job, it was because
the job specifications were written with the education in mind
and not the converse. This was basically the situation when
merit-recruitment to the bureaucracy was conceived. In general,

[1] A. H. Halsey, 'Higher Education', in *Trends in British Society since
1900*, ed. A. H. Halsey (London, 1972), 203, 216.

[2] E.g., Stephen F. Cotgrove, *Technical Education and Social Change*
(London, 1958).

the civil service examinations were based on the curricula of Oxford and Cambridge, or there were, as for those trying out for the India Civil Service, variations in existing programmes of study to which the universities could readily adjust without compromising cherished educational values.

The concern with breadth or general education is still present, therefore, however much attenuated, as the drive towards specialism and occupational professionalism continues. A second traditional concern of liberal education connected with the dream of a good life can also be presently detected and occasionally gives pause for thought: the belief that the end of a liberal education must be to live in harmony with oneself and with society.

To be at ease in the world was to be civilized. That is why, despite its classicism and neoclassicism, eighteenth-century England was never much interested in the philosophy of consolation, in stoicism or stoic writers, except perhaps to use Cato as a model for self-control and virtue. Members of a progressive, enlightened society, it was reasoned, have no need to scorn the world, as it was in the world that a balanced character was formed. The Georgian fallacy was perhaps to attribute too much to secular forms of education, to fly too high with wings of wax.

To live in harmony with oneself was to develop all aspects of character, body as well as mind, and to know society well. This is why the eighteenth-century university failed to achieve a reputation for itself; the education it provided was regarded as one-sided and unrelated to society. The result of the revival of the university in the nineteenth century was not to bring it back into the world, but to allow it to recreate itself as an acceptable alternative world. Since there was no consensus in the Victorian age that living in the world produced the requisite moral education, parents (a particular group of them) were quite willing to have the university become an ivory tower, a place to safeguard the innocence of youth, a special 'culture' against which to assess values outside. This was never true, or as true, of London and the civic universities, although to some extent it was true of Durham; for in the new foundations of the nineteenth century professional and vocational forms of education not only mixed with liberal ones, they were the reasons for their beginnings and consequently the reasons for donnish condescension.

The Georgian theory of self integrated with society may today be found flickering in behavioural schools of psychology. One group of social scientists asks us to work backwards from ends to means, again in order to achieve that co-ordination between the individual and society missing from the modern industrial world where work and social alienation are prevalent. Why not have, if not exactly a New Cortegiano (to pinch a happy expression of G. M. Young's), then at least some model appropriate to the dynamic conditions of contemporary culture? Why not start with a clear definition of the social type or personality required, with 'anticipated behavioural outcomes', and 'manipulate' the student—again to use behavioural language—to produce desired ends? After all, working by analogy, surely this is why vocational education succeeds? The ends are explicit, the goals are known, conflicts are avoided as well as certain kinds of ethical questions. Above all, the student knows where he or she is going.

The romantic revolution, which the nineteenth century and not the Georgians gave us—for individualism, as Werner Jaeger so wisely understands, was never humanism[1]—will not so easily permit the overthrow of the notion of self-development. *Pace* Matthew Arnold, individual self-realization developed from traditions of revolt. The subordination of personality to something impersonal—to job, or society or even knowledge—has periodically produced defiance and the demand for an education more satisfying to the emotions or more flattering to the ego. Putting this for the present aside, however, there is still a philosophical difficulty in proceeding behaviourally from ends to means in liberal education, for ends begin in society, and society is always to some degree in movement, and never so much as now. How can we proceed backwards from ends, how can we 'anticipate behavioural outcomes', when ends are in flux and outcomes uncertain? The nineteenth century preferred an intellectual approach to liberal education because it saw that a society transforming itself and abandoning common cultural values would have as many character formation theories as there were schoolmasters with moral vision. The decision to concentrate on intellect no doubt produced difficulties, but faculty discipline at

[1] Werner Jaeger, *Paideia*, I (New York, 1970), Introduction.

least provided the educational enterprise with unity and direction. In retrospect the Victorian decision seems reasonable. For the historian there can be no ends, only means. The celebrated acorn never becomes an oak but is none the less always growing and changing its form.

Bits and pieces of the Georgian ideal of a liberal education survived the nineteenth century and exist today. But bits and pieces of a tradition will always survive, to become part of the texture of another culture, to mix with altogether new aims and ideals; and in the process new meaning must emerge, for old meaning cannot. Fragments of the past, broken from their historical context, do not recombine to approximate their original form. If every word, value, and idea associated with liberal education carries a different meaning today than it once did, where is the traditional continuity? The Hassidic tale of how a tradition becomes in time a memory states the problem profoundly and has been beautifully retold by Joseph Levenson in his study of Confucian ideals.[1] Gradually a society loses contact with the meaning of its past culture. Uncertain of what was essential, it cannot decide what to keep or leave out. Or even when conscious of its choices, a society may reject past values on the grounds that they are no longer pertinent; or, if pertinent, no longer morally acceptable. Thus the phrase 'polite education' has disappeared. The efforts the Georgians thought they were making to be civilized and to be humane have been repudiated by their descendants in the twentieth century. In contemporary England, Georgian civility is no more than snobbery. The Georgian dislike of the pedant is cited as an example of their dilettantism, and the word is rarely used to expose its roots in 'delight'. Even humanism itself is often identified with a particular style of behaviour and is therefore suspected of harbouring class bias. Self-restraint, the pre-eminent mark of the civilized man, the quality which more than any other drew him away from his brute instinct, has also a class dimension, for precisely the sentiment expressed in this quotation from an Oxford don who taught at Blackheath School in the late nineteenth century: English boys 'regard displays of anger and

[1] Joseph R. Levenson, *Confucian China and Its Modern Fate*, III (Berkeley and Los Angeles, 1965), 124–5.

passion as characteristics of the socially inferior'.[1] And 'Taste' too has fallen a victim to democracy, as well as to Victorian seriousness. 'The feeling induced by what is called a "liberal education" ', wrote Ruskin, 'is utterly adverse to the understanding of noble art; and the name which is given to the feeling —Taste, Goût, Gusto,—in all languages indicates the baseness of it, for it implies that art gives only a kind of pleasure analogous to that derived from eating by the palate.'[2]

In the course of a long development, the meaning of a liberal education turned upside down. A deep discontinuity occurred— a revolution really—in the historical relationship between society, education, and self. The Georgian ideal of sociability, liberality, and civility was peremptorily dismissed. No room was found for it in the cerebral conception of a liberal education that followed. The Golden Rule, neither seeking nor causing pain— this is not even indirectly implied in the critical, truth-seeking ideal of a liberal education. The Georgians were worried that if men were not civil, they would become testy, melancholic, and anti-social. But that is the special fear of a leisured class. Work is the historical antidote to melancholy, hystericks, low spirits, vapours, and the Spleen.

Finally, we must conclude that the process of cultural transmission is bewildering. There is no certain way to guarantee the survival of past values. All traditions are truly selective, as it is common to say; but it ought to be more common to say that what survives from a tradition is most often phrase and form. Perhaps this is fortunate, for painful transitions are thereby eased. But meaning itself changes continually, as do values, and both change radically. The integrity of the past is fragile and shatters easily, and only the whole can give meaning to the parts. What we think we have taken away does not survive. Flowers cut from their scape and separated from their sustaining roots last only a short time. But the flowers live on in the memory, the remembrance of a thing past. *That*, in a deep cultural sense, has always been the history of a liberal education.

[1] G. B. Grundy, *Fifty-five Years at Oxford* (London, 1945), 44.
[2] Excerpted in Robert L. Herbert, *The Art Criticism of John Ruskin* (New York, 1964), 167.

Index

Index

liberal education—cont.

melancholy, 83–6; and work ethic, 86, 121–2, 206; and recreations, 86–7; importance of women to, 87–90; separation of ends and means within, 100–1, 119, 123; disappearance of Georgian theory of, 101, 117–32; ambiguities within Georgian theory of, 102, 110–7, 122–3; importance of religious revivals to, 117–8; and breadth, 123–5, 152–3, 173, 191–2, 202–3; amateur ideal of, 123; and faculty psychology, 126, 133, 161; revival of character formation, 133–45; universal knowledge, 146–57, 168–9, 176, 183; Matthew Arnold restates Georgian ideals, 149–50; definition of affected by industrialism, 146–57; eighteenth-century view of 'invention', 158–64; and new knowledge, 164–73; truth, 169–73, 195 *passim*; and science, 169–73; and 'idea' of a university, 190–1; contradictions within, 193, 193n, 195–206; question of continuity of, 199 *passim*; *see also* art, classics and classical education, examinations, France, Germany, Italy

liberality, *see* liberal, sociability

literature, *see* art

Locke, John, 50–1, 58, 70–1, 75, 79–80, 127–8

logic: scholastic use, 13, 25; Ramist logic, 79; university examinations, 46, 78–80, 124; *see also* rhetoric

London: wealth of, 26, 56–7; importance to liberal education, 32–9; population growth, 32, 37; and royal court, 33–5; and provinces, 33–4; as example of civilization, 34; lord mayor's show, 35; and cosmopolitanism, 36; importance of intellectuals

to, 36–7, 38n, 56–7; city versus country, 37; romantic protest to, 38–9; rejection by Oxford, 39; and 'Taste', 50–8; and sociability, 62, 67, 74; relation to changes in spoken English, 64, 66; servant problem in, 71–2; literacy rate of women in, 88; in the 1790s, 106

London University (and University College, London), 39, 139, 143, 178, 180, 191, 199, 203

Lowenthal, Leo, 50, 73

'luxury', 30

Macaulay, Thomas Babington, 93

madness (insanity), *see* melancholy

Maitland, Frederic, 182–3

Malthus, Thomas, 91

Mandeville, Bernard, 68

manners: kinesic, 15; influence of French on, 15; relation to polite education, 26; London influence on, 38; effect of classical education on, 43 *et seq.*; and mimetic doctrine, 48–9; and courtesy book, 60–1; and correct speaking, 65–6, 113; survival and limits of in the nineteenth century, 118, 133, 136–45; *see also* civility, civilization, liberal education, women

Mannheim, Karl, 89

Marinetti, Filippo Tomasso, *Futurist Manifesto*, 172

Mason College, Birmingham, 139

mathematics, 76, 120, 119–24; *see also* examinations

medicine, 98, 181

melancholy, 83–6, 175, 206; *see also* retirement theme

merit, *see* career, civil service, patronage system, Oxford University, Cambridge University

Meyerson, Martin, 193n

Mill, John Stuart, 128

Millar, John, 24

mimetic doctrine, 47–9, 168–73;